Pioneers of Billerica

Settling the Shawshine Wilderness: 1654-1660

CAMBRIDGE, MARCH 7, 1643-4.

BILLERICA, MAY 30, 1655.

Written by Shirley Moore Barnes
Published by The Billerica Historical Society
2005

Published in the United States by
The Billerica Historical Society
www.billericahistorical.org

ISBN 0-9772673-0-X

Table of Contents

The Founding Fathers of Billerica

Pioneers of Billerica • Settling the Shawshine Wilderness: 1654-1660

Table of Maps

Presentation

The founding fathers have been grouped according to the following categories, below:

for emigration to America –
for owning a garrison-house – 🏠
for service in the militia – ✪
for involvement in witchcraft – 🧙
for injury or death in the Indian Wars – ↘

Emigrated to America

Baldwin
Bird
Chamberlaine
Champney, R.
Croe
Danforth
Farley
Foster
French, J.
French, W.
Hamlet
Hill, Jr.
Hill, Sr.
Jefts
Kidder
Kitterige
Moore
Parker, James
Parker, John
Parker, Robert
Patten, T.
Pattison
Poulter
Rogers
Shedd
Sheldon
Sternes
Tay
Toothaker
Webb
Whiting

Garrison House

Croe
Crosby
Danforth
Farley
Foster
Hill, Jr.
Kidder
Parker, James
Patten, T.
Patten, W.
Pattison
Whiting

Killed by Indians

French, J.
Parker, James's
wife and sons
Rogers' 2 sons
Kinsley's wife

Served in Militia
✪

French, J.
French, W.
Hill, Jr.
Kemp
Kidder
Parker, James
Sheldon

Accused of Being a Witch
🧙

Chamberlaine's wife
Durrant
Toothaker and wife

In addition, within the biographical sketches, each individual's name has been written in the handwriting of the 17th century. This handwriting was primarily influenced by the style of writing used in Elizabethan England. Many of the men in this book did not know how to write their names and therefore used a mark when needed. Wherever a signature was located in a primary document, the form was copied onto the pages of the book and marked with a star to indicate its authenticity. ★

Pioneers of Billerica • Settling the Shawshine Wilderness: 1654-1660

Key to Abbreviations:

b.	born	emig.	emigrated (to the United States)
bp.	baptized	m.	married
bu.	buried	@	approximately
c.	circa (about that time)	-----	date unknown
d.	died	--------	name or location unknown
dy	died young	(--------)	maiden name unknown
		[ ]	reference

Southeastern Section of Cotton Mather's Map 1702 (1696)

Original size 14.75"x 11.87"– Scale reloated on this copy.

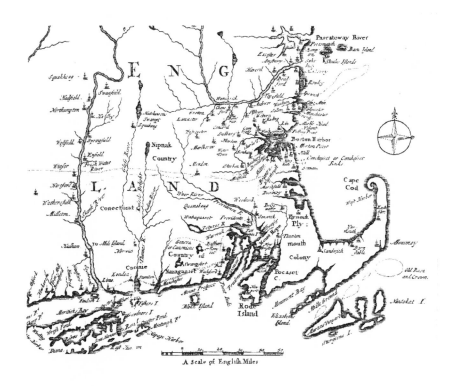

A Scale of English Miles

Pioneers of Billerica • Settling the Shawshine Wilderness: 1654-1660

MAP INDEX

1 York
2 Lincoln
3 Skirbecke
4 Billercay
5 Finchingfield
6 Ipswich
7 Cambridge
8 London
9 Halstead
10 Bath
11 Chester
12 Warwick
13 Exeter
14 Plymouth
15 Dorchester
16 Edinburgh
17 Dublin

GREAT BRITAIN AND IRELAND

Pioneers of Billerica • Settling the Shawshine Wilderness: 1654-1660

New England Settlements

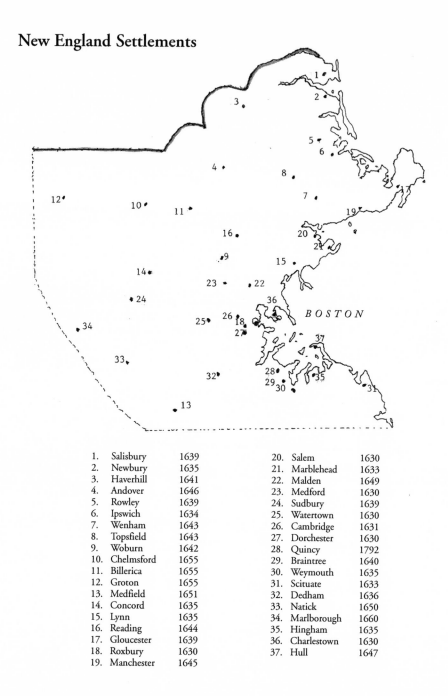

BOSTON

1.	Salisbury	1639	20.	Salem	1630
2.	Newbury	1635	21.	Marblehead	1633
3.	Haverhill	1641	22.	Malden	1649
4.	Andover	1646	23.	Medford	1630
5.	Rowley	1639	24.	Sudbury	1639
6.	Ipswich	1634	25.	Watertown	1630
7.	Wenham	1643	26.	Cambridge	1631
8.	Topsfield	1643	27.	Dorchester	1630
9.	Woburn	1642	28.	Quincy	1792
10.	Chelmsford	1655	29.	Braintree	1640
11.	Billerica	1655	30.	Weymouth	1635
12.	Groton	1655	31.	Scituate	1633
13.	Medfield	1651	32.	Dedham	1636
14.	Concord	1635	33.	Natick	1650
15.	Lynn	1635	34.	Marlborough	1660
16.	Reading	1644	35.	Hingham	1635
17.	Gloucester	1639	36.	Charlestown	1630
18.	Roxbury	1630	37.	Hull	1647
19.	Manchester	1645			

Pioneers of Billerica • Settling the Shawshine Wilderness: 1654-1660

Index to Properties of the Founding Fathers and Present Street Names

Map of Billerica reproduced from Rev. Henry A. Hazen's Book, The History of Billerica, MA

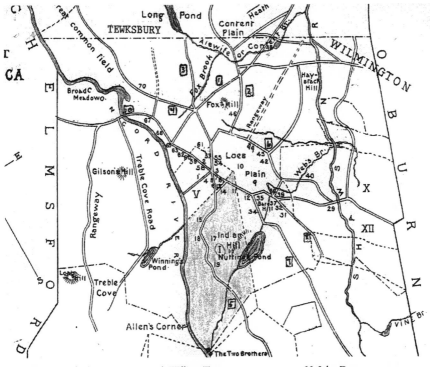

1 Jonathan Danforth	34 William Tay	66 John Durrant
3 Gouldin Moore	35 Simon Crosby	67 William Haile
4 James Kidder	36 William Hamlet	70 Roger Toothaker
5 John Rogers	37 Thomas Foster	I Dudley Farm
6 Daniel Shed	39 Christopher Webb	X Church Farm
7 Thomas Patten	40 John Parker	XII Champney Farm
9 Joseph Tompson	42 Samuel Kemp	
10 Peter Bracket	43 John Marshall	**Streets**
12 William Chamberlaine	46 Stephen Kinsley	
13 Reverend Samuel Whiting	55 John Sheldon	1 Salem Road
14 John Sternes	57 John Poulter	2 Andover Road
15 George Farley	58 John Baldwin	3 Pond Street
16 Henry Jefts	59 James Pattison	4 Rogers Street
17 William French	60 Thomas Hubbard	5 Concord Road
18 Ralph Hill, Sr.	61 John Trull	6 Allen Road
19 Ralph Hill, Jr.	63 Simon Bird	7 Lexington Road
29 Richard & Samuel Champney	65 William Patten,	8 Wyman Road
32 John Kittredge	John Bracket	9 River Street
		10 Boston Road (3A)

Pioneers of Billerica • Settling the Shawshine Wilderness: 1654-1660

Acknowledgements

The development of this book on the forefathers of Billerica, Massachusetts, has been an exciting, stimulating and rewarding experience, for these special people were the nucleus of this town. Locating genealogical and historical material encompassed research in libraries and archival repositories throughout Essex, Middlesex and Sussex Counties, as well as multiple trips to the New England Historic Genealogical Society in Boston. The more I delved into the lives and concerns of these men and their families, the more I saw each person in their unique individuality, but also as a reflection of seventeenth century New England society and its crises. These people created the circle of life in this historic community.

The effort has also provided me with the privilege to work with the president and Board of the Billerica Historical Society. Their keen interest in preserving and illuminating the history of Billerica is a validation of the people who enriched this town with their hard work, strong ethical and moral values, and their willingness to create a place of goodwill for all generations with responsible government.

In particular, I would like to thank the Billerica Historical Society President Robert Kinsman for his interest and encouragement of the proposed book and Board Member David D'Apice for his contribution of photos, maps, memorabilia and graphic creativeness.

A special mention is given to Maria Seminatore, who encouraged me to pursue the book's development and shared some of her own research material with me.

I am most grateful to my family, both close and extended, who have listened to me share my delight and sense of privilege regarding this research. Most importantly, I thank my daughter Ellen Lawrence-Barnes in Arizona who volunteered to take on the task of typing this book for printing. She has diligently persevered in this endeavor, coped with my sometimes-illegible handwriting, and assisted astutely with editing and proofreading of material. Her interest and inquiries about the people and the time often led to a deeper clarification of the early history of Billerica.

Preface

As the waves of immigrants arrived from England at the Massachusetts Bay coastal communities in the mid-1600's, such as Plymouth, Weymouth, Cambridge and Salem, and took up properties and jobs, these towns began to look for inland tracts of land to offer new settlers. Some first-comers were ready to move too, for they yearned for more available farm or meadow land, perhaps more forest, lower taxes, or they desired a new minister or church organization. It was a time of opportunity for some, and usually a positive change in status or income for many others.

The Governor John Winthrop and his assistant Thomas Dudley believed their mission in the Massachusetts Bay Colony was to found a Christian nation with its own self-government, to bring into being taxation only for cause and with representation, and to have a bill of rights and freedom for all men. However, the religious foundation of the colony was the center of political pressures and problems.

Cambridge, MA organized in 1631, was most prestigious with Harvard College, and benefited from a strong intellectual and wise society. The community leaders debated for over 20 years the political and financial necessity of incorporation of a new township to the north and west, which they called Shawshine. This township was finally designed between the Merrimac and Concord Rivers and all the Shawshin River lands. Winthrop and Dudley acquired tracts for themselves and for the president of Harvard College and other well endowed friends and associates.

Two by two or three, enterprising men and their families found their way into the Shawshine expanse by Indian path or by use of the Shawshin or Concord Rivers. Small cabins with one or two rooms were set up; at first with a cow, horse or sow in the rough lean-to for protection from the wild animals in the area.

The early tracts were on the Dudley Farm and the Concord River in present day Billerica, with a secondary settlement at the confluence of roadways at the center of town. The first newcomers were Henry Jefts and his family in 1653, followed by eight other families the following year.

Thomas Dudley's grant was a primary focal point for the acquisition of modest farms with 12 lots each of 100-125 acres, beginning at the large boulders called "Two Brothers" on the east bank of the Concord River. Governor Winthrop's property, which was primarily meadow, lay to the southeast.

On 17 February 1654, the Court in Cambridge ratified an agreement between Cambridge and its 30,000-acre separating township Shawshine. However, the small group of settlers requested their new community lands be called Billercay, reminiscent of the villagers' homeland in eastern England, particularly Billercay.

Pioneers of Billerica • Settling the Shawshine Wilderness: 1654-1660

The church in Cambridge gave a 400-acre grant to Billerica, with the Dudley Farm a dividing point between the grant and the village, and Charnstaffe Lane, the road in between. House lots, 20-30 acres in size, were granted to person of good character, who would be harmonious with others as well as having a certificate of testimonial from their previous towns. In addition to home lots, all residents would benefit from the common lands–usually meadow, but later upland was available.

A large contingent of newcomers came from Braintree, MA and an even larger number from Cambridge, but other families removed from Woburn, Charlestown and Watertown, MA. A few of the group arrived directly from England.

It is believed Jonathan Danforth built the first house in 1654 in the center of the village on the north side of River Street and Boston Road. By 1660, there were 40 families in the area. Frequently these families were related, such as father and son or through inter-marriage following death from childbirth, accident or disease.

Out of necessity, the founding fathers cleared the virgin forest with its gigantic hardwood trees to lay the foundation for a house or barn. The cut trees were the cornerstones and walls of their homes and barns. Roads had to be laid out and planed, and bridges constructed over streams and the large Concord River. In the meantime, the earmarked cattle had to be taken to the meadow to graze, then to be milked, and the butter to be churned. Hunting and woodcutting were also necessary for warmth and food. Fields needed plowing and planting for corn and oats for the animals' feed and vegetables and poultry raised for the family table.

Unless one was well to do and could afford someone else to do the physical work, the planter, farmer or blacksmith seldom pursued relaxing or fun activities. Quite simply, work was never done. During the winter, the working man found part time employment with another or with the town to earn some "hard money." Some of their income had to be used in barter or sale of leather work, clothes and shoes with small wooden heels.

These hardy men—rich or poor—yearned to acquire as much land as they could for reasons of status as they knew it in England or to will to their children on their deaths. As leaders in their homes and in the town, their Puritan beliefs were central to their families' lives. Fathers were expected to be the disciplinarians and to uphold the rules and beliefs of the community. They would punish villagers with severity who disturbed the peace, gossiped against their neighbors, were slothful, neglected their families or abused their wives. Some lenience was allowed about having babies in less than nine months if the couple got married, for men needed to know their wives could be fruitful.

The word of God was an everyday reality of their lives and an all day marathon on Sundays. They trusted in their scripture and in the minister's word, for they had little knowledge of scientific reasoning. Their minds were open to opinions and other than rational conclusions, for many things that happened could be interpreted as the work of the Devil, "signs," witchcraft or animosity from another or direct punishment by God.

The men's wives were to be kindly, hard-working and of moral virtue. They were expected to cope with very difficult everyday tasks, to raise the children with serenity, and to be firm in their religious faith. Women were without doubt the mainstay of the homes, an intense position to hold with the 18 hour day's work.

The 45 founding fathers of Billerica, MA were all married at least once and most had children. In any family, many of the children did not survive to adulthood. Most of the women depended on their first-born children to help with the home responsibilities. The birth and baptism of a new baby was a gift from god, but a new "gift" every year played havoc with a woman's physical health. Prenatal care was unheard of and many women suffered miscarriages or gave birth to a child that had no chance for life beyond a few days.

We know little more than birth, marriage and death dates of the women these men married, for as a rule they did not leave personal records and wills. Some were called upon to be executrix to their husbands' wills and some were included in deeds. Out of necessity, within a few months following widowhood, the woman would marry again to support her children and herself. Intermarriage was common in Billerica, as it was in other communities at this time, and close familial ties were broadened.

Just as with their husbands, most women did not express the emotional turmoil or grief they felt, but kept their own counsel. Surely there were women in Billerica who had special skills such as midwifery, candle making, spinning and weaving, or baking the tastiest pies for the church meeting. Unfortunately, we do not know their names.

The three women who achieved an unnatural fame were accused of being witches in the Salem craze: Martha (Allen) Carrier, her sister Mary (Allen) Toothaker and Rebecca (Shelly/Addington) Chamberlaine. There has not been an adequate explanation for the ferocity of this craze. Some historians attribute malodorous wheat or voodoo imprecations from the Islands, and the hysterical culture for females as the basis for the mania. Reverend Cotton Mather wrote a compelling book on "Memorable Providences" that exacerbated the irrational and nonsensical ideas that sprang forth to give allowance for these vicious trials.

The New England colonies were a religious people, and between the superstitions that lay behind their anxieties and the theology of the minister's preachings to warn about Satan and hell fire, the communities were in jeopardy for the destructive events of the Salem trials.

Many of the Billerica men were artisans or skilled in activities that benefited themselves or the community at large. John Kittredge, for example had knowledge of healing and convalescence; Jonathan Danforth was a surveyor; Thomas Patten built a sawmill; John Rogers was a baker; and the men of the Thomas family were blacksmiths.

Pioneers of Billerica • Settling the Shawshine Wilderness: 1654-1660

This group of founding fathers was between the ages of 22 and 60 years, and was notably self-reliant, tough and high achievers. They believed in public service and helping their fellow man, but especially believed their work should be the main activity of their daily lives. Among themselves, as friends or associates, they especially enjoyed discussing or repairing problems that needed to be fixed.

The first minister in town was the Puritan Reverend Samuel Whiting, Jr., whose house was built and ready for him in 1658, along with the promise of £40 or more a year. In 1659, the community agreed to construct a humble meeting house, 30 feet long by 24 feet wide of boards and a thatched roof. John Parker was the primary builder of the church.

In 1679-80, the meeting house was shingled and a gallery put in to accommodate the church members. But in 1694, even this improvement forced the community to rebuild a new structure with two sets of stairs and a high pulpit.

Reverend Whiting was influential in the Massachusetts Colony as a moderator of the Synod to agree to the baptism of church members' children, and confirm that this baptism gave them rights as citizens. He ministered in Billerica for 56 years, was considered a wise and learned council, and held the word of God with great praise.

Service in the military was expected of all able-bodied fellows. Many of these men reached some prominence in their skills in defending their town, especially in a disastrous trek to Quebec and the two terrible Indian Wars of 1675/6 and 1692/3. James Kidder, one of the founders, died from wounds after the war of 1676. The impact of the Indian hostilities was even more frightful for their wives and children.

The early colonists usually found the local Indian tribes, such as the Wamesit, Nipmjcks and Nachobah, friendly and helpful, but as there were no laws to protect the natives, the wildlife and their property, resentments and resistance increased tensions between both groups. The anxieties in the Billerica community led to the building or strengthening of 11 homes as garrison-fortifications for the families of the town in the event of an uprising. The Hill, Patten, Danforth, Kidder, French, Farley and Rev. Whiting homes were among the safe havens for families and soldiers.

A little over 50 years after the initial settlement at Plymouth, MA tensions reached crisis point for the tribes living in southern Maine, throughout Massachusetts and south to the Narragansett Bay. Once a friend of the Plymouth Pilgrims, King Philip (Metacom), a Wampanoag Indian, turned against the settlers, and perhaps with as many as 15,000 tribesmen, erupted ferociously to attack town after town in New England. Billerica was initially spared, but over half of the other towns were plundered in Massachusetts.

King Philip's War ended the major retaliatory acts of the Indians; however, tensions continued as well as anxieties in the communities. Mary Toothaker, one of the "witches," had nightmares about Indians raiding her home, which was very vulnerable with its location on the north edge of Billerica. At the Salem Trials, she declared she made a covenant with the Devil as a protection for her and her family in May of 1692. On 1 August 1692, the Indians swept into the community and killed at least six people. They returned a few days later and burned the Toothhaker home down, which was deserted with Roger dead and Mary in prison.

To further her nightmare, in 1695, Billerica was attacked again. This time Mary Toothaker was killed and one of her daughters captured. Some captive children were absorbed into Indian families, traded as slaves, sold to planters in the Caribbean, or trafficked to the French in Montreal, where priests baptized them into the Catholic faith. Some of the girls were servants there; a few were lucky enough to marry. It was rare for one of the former captives to escape and return to New England.

Billerica became one of the largest townships in Middlesex County in a 75-year span, with an increase in population that allowed new towns such as Chelmsford, Bedford, Tewksbury and Wilmington to spring forth from its center. Many of the children and grandchildren of the founding fathers flourished as they made their homes in Billerica, or moved out to spread their faith and civilization to settlements in Connecticut, New Hampshire and Vermont.

This book presents the lives, work, wives and children of 45 founding fathers from the years 1654-1660. Some of the families stayed but a year in town; and Elder Champney and John Crowe did not reside here at all. However, the others were the architects, Puritan leaders and dedicated creators of the delightful, historic family town of Billerica, Massachusetts.

Shirley Moore Barnes

Introduction

2005 is a most significant anniversary for the historic town of Billerica, Massachusetts, which blossomed from the Shawsheen Wilderness 350 years ago. The early settlers of 1654-1660 were 45 enterprising men who signed the Cambridge Agreement and established the backbone of this community with their families. They were people who established the religious, political and social structure with their courage, hard work and determination. Over the long span of three and one half centuries, the town has weathered crises of multiple causes and severity, yet can be recognized today for its culture, industry, safety and benevolence towards others.

This book is devoted to sharing the biographies of these 45 men and including the names of their wives and children in the first generation. In most cases, the biographies are brief for the paucity of available information and because the forefathers were "common folk" or common people. The individual may or may not be listed in church or vital records; he may not have had a will or a deed; his arrival in this country more than likely was not recorded, and his name could have been spelled in such a way it would not be found by the researcher. Untold numbers of records have been lost, even if they did exist, through fire, water damage, rodent destruction, war and error in thinking the material was not worth saving.

A few of the men achieved some fame in their employment or lifestyle, such as John Croe, Roger Toothaker and Jonathan Danforth. Jacob Brown, who was considered by other Billerica historians to be missing, deserved a wealth of research, and the hypothesis of his history is presented for review.

The original research developed from Henry Hazen's excellent rendering of Billerica's early chronicle and its peoples in the History of Billerica. However, the book is considered a secondary source of information as are the many family histories reviewed and researched. The bibliography of this book contains both the primary and secondary sources used to write the stories and form the genealogical charts of their families.

These settlers of Billerica were resolute in their determination to succeed with their work, to live with God's blessing, to cope with incredible hardships and adversity, and to give their children and grandchildren wealth in land and coin, as well as the skills needed to continue to build the strength and blessings of this community.

To understand these forefathers and to accept their wisdom and their frailties, is to enrich our own lives, for these pioneers put down roots that enhance our own self-understanding and the historic town of Billerica.

Pioneers of Billerica • Settling the Shawshine Wilderness: 1654-1660

Founding Father

JOHN BALDWIN

m.   ——, Mary Richardson, daughter of Mary & Thomas Richardson
b. 17 Sept. 1638, Woburn, MA
d. After 1687, ————

Children	Born	Married	Died
1. Mary	——	——	1 Feb. 1658, Billerica, MA
2. Mary	28 July 1659, Billerica, MA	——	1 Aug. 1659, Billerica, MA
3. Mary	11 Apr. 1663, Billerica, MA	——, Henry Jefts	22 Sept. 1703, Billerica, MA
4. John	25 Sept. 1665, Billerica, MA	1689/90, Sarah Heywood	6 Apr. 1736, ————
5. Jonathan	28 Jan. 1667, Billerica, MA	1695, Mary French	————
6. Susanna	14 May 1670, Billerica, MA	——	8 Sept. 1675, Billerica, MA
7. Thomas	26 Mar. 1672, Billerica, MA An Ensign	——, Sarah French	12 Dec. 1747, Billerica, MA
8. Phebe	7 Feb. 1675/6, Billerica, MA	——	24 Mar. 1675/6, Billerica, MA
9. Susanna	14 Apr. 1677, Billerica, MA A Lieutenant	——, Joseph Hill	15 Jan. 1758, Billerica, MA
10. Phebe	7 Feb. 1679, Billerica, MA	——, Roger Toothaker A doctor	19 Sept. 1736, Billerica, MA

Pioneers of Billerica • Settling the Shawshine Wilderness: 1654-1660

John Baldwin

b.   *1622, ?Devon, England*
emig.   *1635 on the ship "Pide Cowe" (Pied Cow)*
m.   *15 May 1655, Mary Richardson, Billerica, MA*
d.   *25 September 1687, Billerica, MA*

John Baldwin, age 14, and his brother William, age 9, were transported to New England with a William Harrison, age 55, in July 1635 on the ship "Pide Cowe." They were the only three passengers on board ship. They were certified by a minister and Sir Edward Spencer of Branford.

The historian, Hazen suggested they were brothers of Henry Baldwin of Woburn, who was perhaps six years older than John. The two younger boys may have become orphaned, or in some form of foster care in England, waiting to join their older family member in America.

No employment history has been located, but some confirmation of the relationship with Henry Baldwin has come forth. Henry married a Phebe Richardson in 1649 in Woburn, and John married Mary Richardson 5 May 1655, the daughter of Mary and Thomas Richardson, original settlers of Woburn. Henry Baldwin was a witness to John's will.

John and Mary were married in Billerica and had ten children born in Billerica. Four of these children died young. The family lived on the west side of Boston Road, above River Street after 1657, perhaps living with her family before this date.

Baldwin drafted his will before his death 25 September 1687 in Billerica. It was proven in Boston before Governor Andros 28 March 1688. John left bequests to his wife Mary, sons: John, Jonathan and Thomas, and daughters: Mary Jeffs, Susanna and Phebe Baldwin.

Founding Father
SIMON BIRD

m.

(1) ----, Mary ----
b. ----
d. 1 Apr. 1679, Billerica, MA
Her second marriage was to Henry Jefts - a founding father.

Children	Born	Married	Died

Simon Bird

b.	*1615, England*
emig.	*1635 on the ship "Susan & Ellen"*
m.	*c.1643, Mary -------, Boston, MA*
d.	*7 July 1666, Billerica, MA*

Simon Bird, age 20, arrived in Boston, MA in 1635 as an indentured servant from England. He had sailed on the "Susan and Ellen" with five other young men. On October 6, 1635 Simon was in court with these other men being ordered to be "whipt for running away from their masters and for stealing a boat," plus "diverse other things with them, as also shall give satisfaction to the country for their charges in sending to fetch them home and likewise shall serve their said masters twice as long at the end of their time, as they have been absent from their master's service, by reason of their running away" [Shurtleff, Records of the Governor and Company of the Massachusetts Bay in New England, Vol. I: p. 162].

In the next few years in New England, Bird worked out his service time. In 1643/4, said to be a laborer at Rumley March in Boston, Simon was admitted to the Boston Church. He married Mary ------- about 1643.

The following year on 29 May 1644, Bird became a Freeman, a fellow of good standing with a little property.

However, Bird's good standing in the community was severely tested, when on 5 July 1646, Elder Leveritt excommunicated Simon out of the Boston Church "for filthy unclean dalliances with his maid servant." On 30 April 1648, Simon had repented for his objectionable behaviors and returned to the church community [Anderson, Sanborn, Sanborn, The Great Migration, Vol. I, p. 299].

Simon and Mary were living in Chelsea, MA in 1659 when the couple acquired a 125-acre plot in Billerica. This tract was on the north side of the village, with the house lot a large 52 acres. It was located on the west side of the Boston Road, south of Abbot's Bridge, with the Concord River to his west.

Pioneers of Billerica • Settling the Shawshine Wilderness: 1654-1660

Bird's place was described 10 years later as primarily wilderness and woodlands; although he had farmed, and had considerable meadow and animals.

Simon Bird died 7 July 1666 in Billerica, without children. He left a will written 4 January 1665. His wife Mary was the executrix. She was faced with his bequests in the will and a long line of creditors. A few months after the will was probated, 2 March 1666, Mary married Henry Jefts (3 October 1666).

Bird bequeathed his estate to Mary, and stated that when she died, he wished his "esteemed cousin" Mr. John Wilson and "cousin" Mrs. Mary Danforth of Roxbury to benefit. He was to have £40 and she £20. (These "cousins" were siblings, children of Rev. John and Elizabeth Wilson of Boston). Bird willed Rev. Whiting £10, the Church of Christ at Billerica £10, his landlady Buttolph £5, Mary Bruer of Lynn £5, and Mary Danforth of Billerica 40 shillings. The legacies were valued at £90.40.0 [#1791].

Simon Bird's inventory total was £206.07.6, most of the value in land and animals. He did have two Bibles, a few other books and bees. Henry Jefts became the administrator of Simon's estate when he and Mary married. Henry also acquired the land for his use until Mary's decease. After Mary died in April 1679, Henry and Samuel Manning assumed responsibility for fulfilling the obligations of Simon's will [Middlesex Court File #87].

The value of the Bird estate was then given as £200.12.0, with most of the value in real estate. Jefts had to sell considerable property off to pay the bequests. Rev. Whiting and the Church of Billerica did benefit from the sale.

Founding Father

JOHN BRACKET

Son of Richard Bracket and Alice Blower from England

m.   (1)   ——, Hannah French, daughter of William French of Billerica, MA

b. 16 Feb. 1644, Cambridge, MA

d. 9 May 1674, Billerica, MA

Children	Born	Married	Died
1. Hannah	1 Dec. 1662, Billerica, MA	——, Joseph Bass	——
2. Elizabeth	7 June 1664, Billerica, MA	1691, Daniel Draper	1704, Plainfield, CT
3. Mary	12 Feb. 1665/6, Billerica, MA	1683, Edward Spalding	——, Billerica, MA
4. Sarah	11 Dec. 1667, Billerica, MA	——	——, Billerica, MA
5. Rachel	30 Sept. 1669, Billerica, MA	——	11 Jan. 1671, Billerica, MA
6. Abigail	31 Dec. 1670, Billerica, MA	——	24 Apr. 1673, Billerica, MA
7. Bathsheba	10 Mar. 1671/2, Billerica, MA	——	——, Berwick, ME
8. Samuel	4 Mar. 1672/3, Billerica, MA	——	——, Billerica, MA
9. Marah	9 May 1674, Billerica, MA		

Pioneers of Billerica • *Settling the Shawshine Wilderness: 1654-1660*

John Bracket

bp.   *7 May 1637, Boston, MA*
         (1) 6 September 1661, Hannah French, Braintree, MA
         (2) 31 March 1675, Ruth Ellice Morse, --------
d.   *18 March 1686, Billerica, MA*

The twin brothers Peter and John Bracket came to Billerica in 1660 from Braintree, MA. They were 23 years old, and acquired land next to each other at the intersection of Floyd/Salem and the Boston Roads. The properties were well watered and they were between two brooks, an advantage for household and farm animal needs. John also requested from the town a small piece of land between the highway and his house with an additional small angle at Abbot's Bridge. The town concurred if he would build a bridge at "the durty place."

In addition to Peter joining John in Billerica, their three sisters and husbands also settled here. They were Hannah and Samuel Kingsley, Rachel and Simon Crosby, and Mary and Joseph Thompson.

Their English parents: Richard and Allis Bracket raised the five siblings in Braintree. Richard achieved prominence while holding many town offices. He and Allis were also noted for their strong Puritan beliefs and strictness.

John Bracket took the Oath of Freeman in 1670 and was primarily a farmer during his lifetime. John married twice. His first wife was Hannah French, the daughter of William French of Billerica. They had nine children. Hannah died in childbirth in 1674.

John's second wife was the widow Ruth Ellice Morse of Dedham, MA, who had benefited from her father's will in 1657 when he died in England. John and Ruth had four children together.

Following John's demise, Ruth returned to Dedham with perhaps four or five of their children who were under the age of 16: Samuel, Ebenezer, John, ?Marah and ?Bethia.

John Bracket did not leave a will.

Pioneers of Billerica • Settling the Shawshine Wilderness: 1654-1660

Founding Father

JOHN BRACKET

m. (2) ———, Ruth Ellice, daughter of Joseph Ellice of Dedham, MA
        b. 3 June 1637, Dedham, MA
            Widow of John Morse
        d. 25 Sept. 1692, Dedham, MA

Children	Born	Married	Died
10. John	19 Jan. 1675/6, Billerica, MA	———	24 June 1675/6, Billerica, MA
11. Ebenezer	19 Oct. 1677, Billerica, MA	1712, Abigail Heale	7 Dec. 1750, Dedham, MA
12. John	10 Dec. 1680, Billerica, MA	———, Rebecca ———	5 Feb. 1735, Dedham, MA
13. Bethia	25 May 1682, Billerica, MA	———	———

Pioneers of Billerica • Settling the Shawshine Wilderness: 1654-1660

Pioneers of Billerica • Settling the Shawshine Wilderness: 1654-1660

Founding Father

PETER BRACKET

Son of Richard Bracket & Allis (Blower) Bracket

m. (1) ——, Elizabeth Bosworth, ——

b. 1638, ——

d. 30 Nov. 1686, Billerica, MA

Children	Born	Married	Died
1. Elizabeth	21 Feb. 1662, Billerica, MA	——	27 Feb. 1662, ——
2. Jonathan	22 July 1668, Billerica, MA		11 Mar. 1670, Billerica, MA
3. Elizabeth	30 Apr. 1671, Billerica, MA	——	30 Apr. 1671, Billerica, MA
4. Bethia	10 Apr. 1674, Billerica, MA	——	25 Mar. 1675, Billerica, MA
5. Mary	10 Feb. 1680/1, Billerica, MA	——, Jonathan Hill	13 Feb. 1694/5, Billerica, MA

Pioneers of Billerica • Settling the Shawshine Wilderness: 1654-1660

Peter Bracket

bp. *7 May 1637, Boston, MA*
m. *(1) August, 1661, Elizabeth Bosworth, Braintree, MA*
m. *(2) 30 May 1687, (Sarah Parker) Foster, Billerica, MA*
d. *after 1687, --------*

The twin brothers John and Peter Bracket came to Billerica together in 1660 from Braintree, MA. They were joined by their three sisters and their husbands: Hannah and Samuel Kingsley, Rachel and Simon Crosby, and Mary and Joseph Thompson.

Their parents Richard and Allice Bracket first lived in Boston, MA where Mr. Bracket was employed as a jailer. They resettled in Braintree, where Richard became a leading citizen of the community, holding many offices. As parents, they were recognized for their strict religious views.

At age 23, John and Peter Bracket acquired land for farming next to each other at the center of Loes Plain, east of the Boston Road, Billerica. Until the large trees were cut down by the men and the stumps removed, the land was of little economic value for farming. A small cabin was constructed from the logs, and a lean-to added to the house for a horse, a cow and a pig or two.

Peter would have planted corn first, for it was a staple in every man's diet, ground in a metate or millstone and eaten at breakfast as hominy. It was also fed to the animals. Hay was bountiful in the meadows until snow fell, and even then, some animals could dig their way into the drifts to eat a few morsels of grass.

The next year of two were busy with fencing land for the animals, planting a few orchards, acquiring another animal or two. Of course more corn and now wheat and oats needed to be grown and hopefully not be eaten by the numerous rabbits, mice, skunks, possums and crows.

Founding Father

PETER BRACKET

m.   (2)   ——, Sarah (Parker) Foster
Widow of Dr. Thomas Foster
b. 1640, ————
d. 17 Apr. 1718, Billerica, MA

Children	Born	Married	Died

Pioneers of Billerica • Settling the Shawshine Wilderness: 1654-1660

Hunting and fishing were necessities to supplement the diet and even to acquire a few pelts to sell for a few shillings. Beaver fur was always a good pelt to sell for hats, but moose and bear skins could be used for carriage rides in the cold of winter, and squirrel furs made dandy hats and coat trim for the Gentry's lady.

Peter became a Freeman 30 October 1680 after his last child was born. He could now afford a larger dwelling and maintained a larder with the best of victuals, beer, cider and wine.

He married twice. His first wife was Elizabeth Bosworth, whom he married in Braintree. She died 30 November 1686 in Billerica. They had five children, but only one survived childhood. Even this daughter Mary died at the age of 24 after marrying Jonathan Hill.

Peter married again on 30 March 1687 to the widow Sarah (Parker) Foster, who had been married to Dr. Thomas Foster, a son of the founding father.

In the spring of 1708, Peter received 47 acres in Billerica in a land division. This is the last mention of him found. We do not know the date of his death. Sarah died 18 April 1718 in Billerica.

A Metate, used as a stone tool throughout North America by early settlers.

Pioneers of Billerica • Settling the Shawshine Wilderness: 1654-1660

Founding Father

JOHN BROWNE, alias JEAN LE BRUN
Hypothesis: Parents of Jacob Browne of Billerica, MA
    m. Before 1636, Ales --------
             b. --------
             d. --------

Children	Born	Married	Died
1. Jonathan	------, Isle of Jersey?	28 June 1664, Abyhaile Burrill	1667, shipwreck off Virginia coast
2. John Jr.	bp. 16 Sept. 1638, Salem, MA	1658, Hannah Hubbard	?13 Sept. 1677, Ipswich, MA
3. James	A mariner; served at Kennebec, ME July 1677		
4. Samuel	bp. 7 June 1640, Salem, MA	------	
5. Jacob	bp. 13 Mar. 1642, Salem, MA	9 July 1661, Mary Mattock	Before 1675, Boston, MA
6. James	bp. 13 Mar. 1642, Salem, MA	16 Oct. 1661, ?Mary Taplease	After 1672, Suffolk Co., MA
7. ?Joanne	bp. 17 July 1642, Salem, MA	1664, Hanna Bartholomew	1678-80, Salem, MA
8. Elizabeth	bp. 9 Apr. 1643, Salem, MA	------	------
9. Nathaniel	bp. 14 Apr. 1644, Salem, MA	(1) 1664, Joseph Grafton	------, Salem, MA
		(2) 1673, Samuel Gardiner, Sr.	widow, will 5 June 1693, intestate
	bp. 28 July 1644, Salem, MA	1667, Hannah --------	After 1672, Chebacco, MA

Pioneers of Billerica • Settling the Shawshine Wilderness: 1654-1660

Jacob Browne

b.   *?1635-1641, --------*
m.   *16 May 1661, Mary Tapleafe, Boston, MA*
d.   *-----*

In 1658, Jacob Browne acquired 50 acres and 54 poles (87 feet) of upland in Billerica, along with nine acres and 100 poles (166 feet) of meadow. His house lot seems to have been the lot of 23 acres along the Concord Road, but he was also deeded 21 acres on Loes Plain. Jacob acquired small lots of meadow on the west side of the Concord River, below the falls near the Chelmsford line and on the Shawshin meadow.

In 1659, Browne bought 18 acres in the large common field below the falls, on the east side of the Concord River; and then in the second division of lands, he acquired another 45 acres.

In Boston on 16 May 1661, Jacob married Mary Tapleafe (Taplease, Tapley), whose identity is presently unknown. She may have emigrated alone to New England, or more likely was a sister to Gilbert Tapley of Salem, MA, a mariner Robert Tapleigh of Portsmouth, NH, or related to the Taplifs of Dorchester, MA.

The couple lived in Billerica for a couple of years, for on 1 June 1661, Browne was on a committee with Henry Jefts, Ralph Hills, Sr. "to run the (boundary) Line Nexte to Chelmsford" [Hazen, p. 75].

In 1663, Jacob and Mary left Billerica after deeding a variety of his properties, as well as the Concord Road holding to John Sternes.

During their five-year association with Billerica, perhaps only a few people acquired any knowledge of Jacob or Mary, for even these friends and acquaintances did not leave records about the ages, history and activities of the Brownes. However, from his land holdings, we can conclude that Jacob had some financial assets when he came to this community. By marrying a young lady in Boston after residence here, he probably had known her at an earlier date, and was also familiar with a more urban environment. It seems credible to assume that when the couple left Billerica in 1663, not having found a life here that suited them, they returned to Boston or coastal New England. It was also possible they left the country for the West Indies, or moved to New Jersey, which became a new English colony after 1664.

This researcher did an extensive search in the Boston-Newbury, MA area and in New Hampshire and Maine. New Jersey, New York, Long Island and West Indies records were also researched. Out of this extensive search, only four Jacob Brownes were located in the time period.

The first was Jacob Browne, born in Hampton, NH in 1645, son of John Browne and Sarah Walker. He married Sarah Brooker in 1683 and had a son Samuel, born in 1686. This infant may have been the one who, as an adult, completed probate on his father's estate in Hampton 26 March 1740 (Jacob died 13 February 1740.) This Jacob Browne was a Yeoman and on a jury in a New Hampshire trial in August 1684 with 15 other men. When he died, his estate inventory was £34.0.0 [Probate Record of New Hampshire, Vol. 3, p.779]. In 1704, Browne had land at Great Neck Marsh near James Perkins, Hampton, NH.

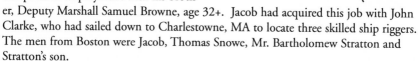

A second Jacob Brown, age 85 in 1737 (i.e. b. 1652) disputed the boundary line between New Hampshire and Massachusetts. A third was Lieutenant Jacob Browne of Ipswich, or the "Hamlet," who died 26 February 1769. These three Jacob Browne's were too young to be the Jacob Browne of this search.

The fourth Jacob Browne was more promising.

This Jacob Browne, age 32+, had a position as an expert ship rigger in 1670 at Greenland, New Hampshire. He was at this place of employment with his brother, Deputy Marshall Samuel Browne, age 32+. Jacob had acquired this job with John Clarke, who had sailed down to Charlestowne, MA to locate three skilled ship riggers. The men from Boston were Jacob, Thomas Snowe, Mr. Bartholomew Stratton and Stratton's son.

Henry Greenland, Walter Barefoot and Robert Marshall of Greenland, NH were in the process of building a ship as joint owners. Their builder was shipwright George Norton of Kittery, Maine. Greenland is a small and lively community west of Portsmouth, NH on the southeastern end of the Great Bay, which flows into the Piscataqua River.

There was foul play on the ship as it was being constructed, and although the text is not entirely clear, a "body" (David Campbill) was arrested for tampering with the construction and rigging of the ship in September 1670. Because of his destruction, Campbill was escorted to Dover, NH and then to the prison in York, ME.

On 2 September 1670, there were more altercations between the owners and builder. Jacob and Sam Browne heard Barefoot say that George Norton would not let Robert Marshall come aboard the ship and so pushed him into the sea. Dr. Greenland attempted to rescue Marshall, and grabbed a pole from Constable John Hole "which he thrust with swearing" towards Norton. On 25 October 1671, Jacob Browne testified in court that "George Norton told me I should not come on board alive. We believed we would have been murdered by him." Samuel Browne concurred [Noyes, Davis, Libby, p. 15, 114].

This writer searched further through deeds, wills, vital statistics and histories from Boston to New Hampshire with the paired names of Jacob and Samuel Browne and the marriage date of Jacob and Mary. Even with the commonality of the Brown/Browne name, however, the combination of two names Jacob and Samuel narrowed the field. It was also soon clear that Jacob was not a common first name.

This scrutiny led to the discovery of a Jacob and Samuel Browne baptized in Salem, MA in 1642, which perhaps poses a more promising theory and concrete relationship to the Jacob Browne from Billerica. However, no concrete evidence has been located to prove this hypothesis.

John and Ales Browne of Salem, MA, parents of Jacob and Samuel, had perhaps nine or 10 children. These two children were baptized on the same day at the First Church in Salem on 13 March 1642. They may have been twins, but it was also very common in the early churches to have more than one child baptized the day the preacher was in the village, since many ministers were on a rotation of congregations. Toddlers and youngsters as well as infants could be baptized.

Not only was John Browne a church member and a proprietor in Salem in 1637, a Freeman in 1638, and a ruling elder in 1660, but he was also a mariner. He was skilled in navigation and able to afford his own vessels to sail along the shores of the American colonies, to the West Indies and abroad. He had to be knowledgeable of the Gulf Stream, prevailing winds and Atlantic storms, but also equipped to sail into estuaries with floating logs or sand bars to reach small wharfs in outlying areas.

In the 17th century, a mariner and ship owner would include on their voyages sons, nephews and even wives. From an early age, the boys would learn how to sail a ship, to oversee ship construction and rigging, and how to make decisions about weather, what products to trade and the secrets of making money in the shipping business. Every mariner knew, however, it was a risky business. In that century, Salem was the most important seacoast town in the colonies. Trade was frequent with other colonies, such as

New Amsterdam/New York, Delaware, Maryland and Virginia, but there was also a triangular trade to England, Holland and France, with a third leg being the West Indies or the African coast for slaves.

The small 40-60 ton ships used to transport goods and people were one-masted sloops or three-masted ketches, strong enough to cope with heavy waves during turbulent weather. The ships were not built for speed, so were very vulnerable to attacks by pirates or armed sloops from France or the Barbary Coast of North Africa. If stopped and over-run, the sailors would be impressed, imprisoned and then sold into slavery. Since the boats also sailed into rivers and bays in wilderness or unsettled areas, the sloops and ketches were open to attacks and fire from American Indians on the warpath.

Every ship owner and master also had to cope with the numerous restrictions of the English government's Acts of Trade. Smuggling became the way of life for many, since the colonists had no intention of stopping their marine commerce. Wealth and power were primary aims for the ship owners, but the people in the seafaring towns depended and benefited as well with jobs, money and goods.

Trade of products from New England increased substantially from the beginning days of the colony. Ships that sailed south carried fish, cider, horses, cows, lumber, wooden bowls, pork and rum made from West Indies molasses. On the return trip from the south, boats carried hogsheads of tobacco, pewter, copper, Indian corn, furs, deerskins and English goods. Voyages to Europe would carry barrels of tobacco or codfish, furs and rum.

Research in the Salem, MA records led to a brief account of a trip to Virginia where John Browne's vessel was wrecked; and he lost both the ship and the cargo. No mention was made of the seamen on board. Few maritime records have survived from these early sailing days in America, and no other details have been located. However, on 6 March 1661/2, Elder John Browne thanked God before the Salem church congregation for allowing him to return safely home after being in great danger from the wreck and the Indians.

A few weeks later, on 6 June 1661, John Browne and two partners, Nicholas Bailhache and John Balach, agreed to have a new vessel built in Salem by William Stephens. In the historical document regarding this agreement, it was noted that John Browne's original name was Jean Le Brun and that Browne and the two merchants were all former Jersey residents.

In this case, Jersey referred not to New Jersey, but the Isle of Jersey, 15 miles west of the coast of France in the Gulf of St. Malo and the English Channel. As one of the Channel Islands, with their long history of changed ownership, it was culturally French, but politically English and Protestant. During the late 16th and 17th centuries, many French Huguenots from the European Continent emigrated into the Islands, bringing with them their strong values for discipline, order, education and skill in knitting lisle stockings acclaimed by the affluent in Europe. The two other important occupations on the Islands were fishing and trade. The Jersey Islanders, like those of Mont St. Michel, had learned to cope with 40-50 foot ebbing tides and surges. Browne was said to be an agent for the Isle of Jersey at Salem, MA [Balleine's History of Jersey, p. 155].

The new ship of Balach, Bailhache and Browne, a two-masted ketch, was to be 68 feet by the keel and 23 feet wide, 9½" under the beam with two decks. It was to be completed by July 1661. The cost was £3.5 for each ton, i.e. "at Mr. Browne's (Browne & Co.) £50 or £100 of New English money" [Perley, Vol. 2, p. 358-9].

In 1671, John Browne was the master of a two-masted vessel of 10-12 tons called a pinke. This ship was primarily a fishing boat and did not have a bowsprit, but had a narrow, overhanging stern. The boat was called the "Pink of Salem."

In 1676, Browne was enlisted to be involved in the "Dutch War," the conflict between New Netherlands and Great Britain. Three of Browne's ships were used: the "Anthony," the "Swallow" and the "Salisbury." The outcome of this war was the British takeover of the Manhattan colony from the Dutch.

On 10 October 1682, (with a new title of status) Mr. John Browne was appointed surveyor for Salem, MA to examine goods aboard ship before unloading.

John Browne left a will in Essex County, MA, written 2 January 1683, probated 24 November 1684 [Essex Co. Pro. Docket #3614, Vol. 2, p. 156-7]. It has been an important document validating some members of his extended family, but also because there is no mention of others. Four of his sons: Jacob, Samuel, John, Jr. and Nathaniel were not mentioned, nor any of their children. His wife Ales probably pre-deceased him, and was not listed in the will. This lack of reference often means these relatives died before him, but it could signify they were alienated from him, he did not know where they were, or they had already benefited from his largesse.

However, in the years 1676-1682, the only three deeds located in the early county records at Salem, MA were to James Browne [1676:Lib. 4:110], Samuel Gardner, Jr. [1676:Lib 4:138] and Hannah Browne [1680:Lib 5:41].

Browne's will stated that he wished his granddaughter Abion to have £20 at age 18 or when she married. His grandson John was to have the house, warehouse, part of the orchard and salt marsh at "Castlehill." The remainder of the estate was to be divided: one half to "daughter Gardner" (i.e. Elizabeth) and one half to the four children of his deceased son James. The causeway, wharf and pond were to be granted and used by "those who live on my land." His son-in-law Samuel Gardiner, Jr. was to be the executor.

This will included a very impressive inventory, but there was no mention of his vessels or the contents of the warehouse. Four properties were noted:

"Castlehill," which he acquired from John Bullock, value £220.

Dwelling house and land, "where Jonathan formerly lived," value £120.

Kitchen and barn, value £90.

Great Hall, adjacent to Dr. Swinnerton's home and land.
Also a Great Yard and mulberry tree. Value £150.

The inventory also listed that he owned pewter, damask curtains, oriental carpets, a large chest, two silver cups, a large Bible, a featherbed bolster and three Great Chairs. The Browne's total inventory amounted to £681.14.3.

Browne's daughter Elizabeth, wife of Samuel Gardiner, Jr., was probably John's caregiver at the time of his death. Elizabeth was first married to Joseph Grafton of Charlestown, MA. After Joseph's death in 1673, she wed Samuel Gardiner. One witness to the will was John Grafton, most likely a brother to her first husband.

It seems feasible to think that John Browne had already transferred ownership of his vessels before his death at age 66. Unfortunately, documents have not been located to verify this transfer, nor vital records to indicate the deaths of his wife or sons. The latest documents on sons: John, Jr., Jacob and Nathaniel were dated at least five years before his passing.

Samuel Browne died before 1675 in Boston, MA. He did not leave a will. He married Mary Mattock in Salem and had four children baptized in Boston: James 1662, Mary 1664, Samuell 1669 and Hannah 1672.

Twice in January 1670, Samuel witnessed deeds of four mariners in Suffolk County: Thomas Summers to Samuel Mattock and Richard Gridley to Robert Marshall [Suffolk County Lib., VII, p. 215, 139]. He also testified before the Judicial Court in Boston 7 March 1671 regarding his role as a grantor [Suffolk County Bk. 32, 1672, #1137].

It is important to note that between 1698 and 1706 in Salem, a Samuel Browne was part or full owner of a number of vessels: the "William," "Adventure," "Greyhound," "Union," "Friendship" and the Brig "Dragon." A Bill of Lading in 1707 for Philip English, the richest man in America at that time, listed English, Captain William Bowditch, William Pickering, Samuel Wakefield and Samuel Browne. Of the 21 vessels that English owned, the sloop "Mayflower" was bound for Virginia or Maryland with salt.

John Browne, Jr. was a mariner, who was impressed into military service at Kennebec, ME in July 1677 in an Indian uprising. According to Ipswich, MA vital records, a John Browne, Jr. died 13 September 1677.

Nathaniel Browne married Hannah -------- in 1667, and in 1678 lived at Chebacco, Essex County, MA. He had a daughter Sarah, born 1668.

The last two references for Jacob Browne were in Suffolk County, MA. He was a witness to a deed 4 August 1671 between mariners Theodor Atkinson and Henry Ellis [Suffolk County Lib. VII:189]. He was also criticized by the court in the second document because he did not read the whole statement to which Gabrigan Boynton bore witness on 26 March 1672 [Suffolk County Lib. 39, p. 413-4]. There is no will for Jacob Browne in Suffolk, Middlesex or Essex Counties, MA, nor is there record of relocating to Rhode Island or Connecticut or perhaps even the Isle of Jersey.

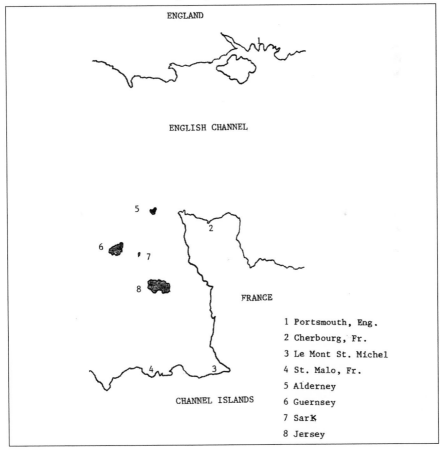

Pioneers of Billerica • Settling the Shawshine Wilderness: 1654-1660

Founding Father

WILLIAM CHAMBERLAINE

m. (1) -----
b. -----
d. -----

Children	Born	Married	Died

Pioneers of Billerica • Settling the Shawshine Wilderness: 1654-1660

William Chamberlaine (signature)

William Chamberlaine

b.	*1619/20, England*
emig.	*1635 on the ship "Hopewell"*
m.	*(1) -----*
m.	*(2) 1648/9, Rebecca Shelley/Addington, --------*
d.	*31 May 1706, Chelmsford, MA*

At age 16, William Chamberlaine embarked on the ship "Hopewell" for New England in September 1635 with 53 other passengers. It was stated in the ship's listing that he was in conformity to the Church of England, and "yt they are no Subsedy men" [Tepper, Passengers to America, p. 35]. It is most likely someone else paid for his passage, and when he arrived in this country, he became a servant to that individual. This may also be why the years between 1635 and 1647 are a blank of information on him. In 1644, he lived in Boston and owned a house and land he acquired from a Francis Smith. In 1648/9, William moved to Woburn, acquiring property as well. Some time during these years, he married for the first time. Details of this marriage are unknown.

About mid/late 1648, William married again. His wife was Rebecca Shelley or Addington. He and Rebecca had 13 children, nearly all born in Billerica. The historian James Savage, stated that two of the sons were born in Concord, MA, but it seems more likely it was Woburn.

In 1652 Williams was deeded Thomas Haman's (Hammond) lot in Billerica. He eventually acquired 11 grants of land in the area comprising at least 200 acres. His property and dwelling house were on the Dudley Farm near the Boston Road, on the south side of the village just above Bare Hill.

William had an investment in this community, and was one of the settlers who went to the Cambridge Court to apply for separation from Cambridge and to all the town Billerica. Among his other activities as a farmer, woodsman, hunter, he was Constable of Billerica in 1673.

His wife Rebecca was a sister to Sarah Shelley, who wrote her will 21 April 1686/7. This will holds a great deal of family information. Sarah forgave "Brother" William

Founding Father

WILLIAM CHAMBERLAINE

m. (2) ----, Rebecca (Shelley) Addington

b. ----

d. 26 Sept. 1692, Cambridge, MA

Children	Born	Married	Died
1. Timothy	13 Aug. 1649, Concord, MA	------	died young
2. Isaac	1 Oct. 1650, Concord, MA	Unmarried	20 July 1681, Billerica, MA
3. William, Jr.	1652, ------	1698, Deliverance Ferguson	20 Jan. 1734, Lexington, MA
4. John	1651-1654, ------	1681, Deborah Jaco	1 Apr. 1712, Billerica, MA
5. Sarah	20 May 1655, Billerica, MA	1676/7, John Shed	17 Jan. 1736, Billerica, MA
6. Jacob	18 Jan. 1657/8, Billerica, MA	------, Experience ------	11 Apr. 1712, Newton, MA
7. Thomas	20 Feb. 1659, Billerica, MA	------, Elizabeth Hammond	July 1724, Newton, MA
8. Edmond	15 July 1660, Billerica, MA	(1) ------, Mary Abbott (2) ------, Sarah Forbush	After 1740, Woburn, MA
9. Rebecca	25 Feb. 1662/3, Billerica, MA	(1) ------, Thomas Stearnes (2) 1699, George Farley	------, Billerica, MA
10. Abraham	6 Jan. 1664/5, Billerica, MA	(1) ------, Elizabeth ------ (2) ------, Mary Randall	After 1686/7, ------
11. Ann	3 Mar. 1665/6, Billerica, MA	Unmarried	After 12 Dec. 1726, Billerica, MA
12. Clement	30 May 1669, Billerica, MA	------, Mary ------	21 Jan. 1754, Billerica, MA
13. Daniel	27 Sept. 1671, Billerica, MA	------, Mary ------	After 1725, Billerica, MA

Chamberlin the debt of £6. She bequeathed to "my sister," his wife Rebecca and her three daughters 20 shillings each and 20 shillings to Cousin John Chamberlin's wife (son of Rebecca and William, i.e. Deborah Jaco Chamberlin).

Deborah, Rebecca and her daughters were to have all of Sarah's wearing apparel (a fine gift in those days) and household goods, except for three small pewter dishes marked "S.S." which she wanted Cousin (niece) Sara Chamberlin Shed's children to have. The remainder of Sarah's estate was bequeathed to Rebecca's eight sons with John and Clement (whom she called cousins, but were nephews) to have 20 shillings apiece more than the others. She also gave Cousin Sarah Shed's children £10, and John and Thomas Chamberlin £10 each. "Kinsmen" Isaac Addington (1674-1715) was the executor of the will.

Rebecca Chamberlaine died 26 September 1692 in "ye prison at Cambridge" [Hazen, p. 196]. There is a lack of other details regarding her internment and death, but we know this was the time of the Salem witchcraft hysteria and trials.

Following her demise, William Chamberlaine moved to Chelmsford, MA. He died there 31 May 1706, 86 or so years old. He did not leave a will.

Founding Father
RICHARD CHAMPNEY

m.   c. 1628, Jane ——, England
b. ——
d. After husband in 1669, ——

Children	Born	Married	Died
1. Sarah	bp. 21 June 1629, Stisted, England	----	died young
2. Ester	bp. 31 Oct. 1630, Stisted, England	(1) ——, Josiah Converse	5 Apr. 1713, Billerica, MA
		(2) 1690, Jonathan Danforth	
3. Joseph	bp. 8 Apr. 1632, Stisted, England	——, Sarah Poole	1656, Billerica, MA
4. Noah	bp. 8 Apr. 1634, Stisted, England	----	died young
5. Samuel, *twins*	Oct. 1635, Cambridge, MA	(1) 1657, Sarah Hubbard	1696, -------
		(2) ——, Ruth M. Green	
6. Mary, *twins*	Oct. 1635, Cambridge, MA	----	died young
7. Sarai	May 1638, Cambridge, MA	1656, William Barrett	21 Aug. 1661, Cambridge, MA
8. Mary	Nov. 1639, Cambridge, MA	1665, Jacob French	1 Apr. 1681, Billerica, MA
9. John	28 May 1641, Cambridge, MA	----	died young
10. Lidea	1643 or 1648, Cambridge, MA	1668, John Hastings	23 Jan. 1691
11. Daniel	9 Mar. 1644/5, Cambridge, MA	(1) 1665, Dorcas Bridge	1691, Cambridge, MA
		(2) 1684, Hepzibah C. Minot	

Pioneers of Billerica • Settling the Shawshine Wilderness: 1654-1660

Richard Champney, Elder

b.	*c.1600-1604, Stisted, Essex, England*
emig.	*July 1635 on the ship "Defence"*
m.	*@1629, England, Jane -------, place unknown -------*
d.	*26 November 1669, Cambridge, MA*

The Ruling Elder of the Cambridge Church was Richard Champney, who first arrived July 1635 in the Massachusetts Bay Colony on the ship "Defence". The following year he and his wife Jane were members of the Puritan Cambridge congregation.

Almost immediately, Richard and Jane acquired three homes in the west end of Cambridge, MA. Year after year, he acquired more land and houses, as a gentleman would do in England. As Elder or Yeoman Champney, he had property in Newtown, Charlestown, the Alewife Meadow, Strawberry Hill in Cambridge and Billerica, MA.

In 1652, before there was much real estate activity in Shawshine, Champney drew Lot #83, which was 350 acres of land. He was clearly very interested in the development of his real estate, for he was one of the men who petitioned the Cambridge Court in 1655 for Shawshine to be separate from Cambridge and be called Billerica. On 10 December 1655, Edward Collins of Medford sold him 500 acres in this community. On 24 November 1665, James Parker and Thomas Chamberline deeded him several more tracts in Billerica, part of the original Dudley Farm. Richard's large landholdings were to the west of the Boston Road and the Shawshin River. To understand how extensive his real estate

Pioneers of Billerica • Settling the Shawshine Wilderness: 1654-1660

was, in the inventory of his estate in 1669, his houses, barns, meadows and woodland were valued at £1,260.

There is little evidence that Richard Champney resided in Billerica, MA. However, three of his children and their families: Ester, Mary and Joseph settled in the village.

Champney was the ruling elder and assisted the minister Rev. Thomas Shepherd at communion in the Cambridge Church. With his above average education, Richard saw to the recopying of the Cambridge Cow Commons line and owned numerous books. He valued education and, at his death, willed 40 acres of land to Harvard College to educate youth with religious literature.

Richard Champney drew up a lengthy will 30 June 1669, probated 21 December 1669 [Middlesex Probate #4240]. He gave his wife Jane the two best rooms in their house, use of their furnishings, a horse, cow and two sheep, while she remained his widow. He also willed her £15 a year. However, if she remarried, she could retain only her own belongings.

Champney bequeathed his daughters Ester Convers, Mary French and Lidea Champney £100 each and the lands acquired in Billerica. The rest of the real estate and property he bequeathed to his sons Samuel and Daniel to be divided in a particular fashion, but Daniel was to have Billerica property and Samuel the Cambridge lands. His inventory total was £1,449.16.0.

Founding Father

SAMUEL CHAMPNEY

Son of Elder Richard and Jane Champney

m. (1) 13 October 1657, Sarah Hubbard, ———
   b. Before 1638, ———

   Her brother Thomas Hubbard married Sarah Ives.
   When Thomas died c.1639/40, his widow married William Hamlet, a founding father.

   d. 1690-1694, ———

Children	Born	Married	Died
1. Samuel	bp. 13 Feb. 1658, Cambridge, MA	———	dy
2. Sarah	17 Feb. 1659, Billerica, MA	1685, James Clark	After father's death, Cambridge, MA
3. Mary	bp. 17 Aug. 1662, Cambridge, MA	1685, David Stowell	1690, Cambridge, MA
4. Easter	14 May 1664, Billerica, MA		31 March 1667, Billerica, MA
5. Samuel	19 Mar. 1666/7, Billerica, MA	———	8 Mar. 1745, Cambridge, MA
6. Joseph	1 Sept. 1669, Cambridge, MA	———, Sarah ———	19 Jan. 1730, Cambridge, MA
7. Richard	20 Aug. 1674, Cambridge, MA	———	Before father, ———

Pioneers of Billerica • Settling the Shawshine Wilderness: 1654-1660

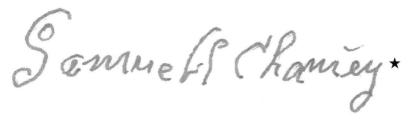

Samuel Champney

b.	*September 1635, Cambridge, MA?*
m.	*(1) 13 October 1657, Sarah Hubbard, Billerica, MA*
	(2) 1690-1694, Ruth (Mitchelson) Green, --------
d.	*@Dec. 1695, Cambridge, MA*

Samuel Champney was the son of Elder Richard Champney of Cambridge, MA who bought a farm of 500 acres in 1655, which became the home of Samuel and his wife Sarah in 1657. In 1669, Samuel sold the large property and dwelling house, located south of the Boston Road adjacent to the Shawshine River. He moved back to Cambridge with his family.

Samuel was a selectman from 1684-1691, and was called Mr. Sam Chame when he surveyed and repaired the Great Bridge over the Charles River in Cambridge.

His first wife was Sarah Hubbard of Watertown, with whom he had seven children. His second spouse was Ruth (Mitchelsen) Green, widow of John Green. He left a will [#4242] that was written 21 September 1690, with a codicil 1 May 1694. This document was proven January 1695/6.

The original will was very detailed, written in both a religious and practical manner. Sarah, his wife for 35+ years, was living, and was to have the liberty of living in his "dwelling house" while she was his widow. He expressed his wish that his executors, sons Samuel and Joseph, provide for her as his widow. He wanted daughter Sarah Clark to have £30 and her two daughters Sarah and Nancy to have £5 each to be paid in cattle and corn. His grandson Samuel Stowell was to have £10 if he lived to be 21, and granddaughter Ruth Stowell £6 on the same condition.

The remainder of the estate was to be given to two sons, with Samuel getting the "mansion house" and multiple properties and Joseph 40 acres and other lands. If one son died, the other would benefit. The postscript was probably added following the death of Sarah and his remarriage.

Ruth was to have use of the rooms in the dwelling house and £4 every year in pork, goods, wood, milk, fruit, etc. However, if she decided to move into town, she was to have £3 in grain, but if she married again, she would only have what she brought with her.

His intent was that Mary's husband David Stowell (deceased in 1690) should not benefit further from the estate.

Pioneers of Billerica • Settling the Shawshine Wilderness: 1654-1660

Founding Father
SAMUEL CHAMPNEY

m. (2) 1690-4, Ruth (Mitchelson) Green, ———
b. 9 Nov. 1638, Cambridge, MA
Daughter of Edward and Ruth (Bushell) Mitchelson. First husband: John Green.
d. 1728, ———

Children	Born	Married	Died

Pioneers of Billerica • Settling the Shawshine Wilderness: 1654-1660

Founding Father

JOHN CROE

m. ——, Elishua ——

b. ——, England

It has been suggested that Elishua may have been John's second wife.

d. 1688, Yarmouth, MA

Children	Born	Married	Died
1. Yelverton	c.1615, England	Before 1642, Elizabeth ——	will 1681, West Yarmouth, MA
2. Elizabeth	c.1617, England	(1) ——, Arthur Perry, Sr.	——
		(2) Before 1654, John Gillet	
		(3) 1657, William Wardwell	
3. John	c.1635, ?Charlestown, MA	c.1656, Mehitable Miller	28 Jan. 1689, Yarmouth, MA
4. Moses	bp. 24 June 1637, Charlestown, MA	——	died young
5. Elishua	——	——, John Gifart	——, Sandwich, MA

Pioneers of Billerica • Settling the Shawshine Wilderness: 1654-1660

John Croe (Crowe, Crowell)

b.	1590, ?Norfolk, England
emig.	1634/5
m.	-----, Elishua --------, England
d.	7 January 1672, Yarmouth, MA

Historians of Billerica recognize the name of John Croe, for he was involved with the dozen or so other negotiators in the winter of 1654 to have the Shawshine settlement secede from Cambridge and become a town called Billerica.

John Croe (Crowe and later Crowell) was a surveyor, and eventually a magistrate who had wealth and standing at Yarmouth on southeast Cape Cod.

John's wife Elishua (--------) came to America in 1634 and bought a family home in Charlestown, MA of Mr. Williams Jennings. She was admitted to the Charlestown Church that year.

Croe emigrated from England to Charlestown, MA in 1635, but sold his property there in 1638 to Mathew Averie. Croe had acquired a bull, which the town 'used' for 1638 as well as four cow commons and other pieces of land, each 45-50 acres each.

Thomas Makepeace of Dorchester, MA was deeded a house and 200 acres of Croe's land near Dedham, MA about June 1641.

John also invested in 53 acres of property in Woburn, but held on to this. It was sold by his granddaughter Deborah Man in March 1704/5. At that time, James Converse was using the land.

John Croe did not acquire land in Billerica, MA.

About 1638, John and his wife decided to resettle on Cape Cod at "Mattacheset" or Yarmouth. The religious body in that community was more liberal, under the leadership of Rev. John Lathrop, who had originally landed at Scituate, MA. Lathrop was beloved by his congregation and Croe moved with the minister and his congregation to the Cape.

John was active at Yarmouth in the town committees 1638/9 and he was one of the men to survey the first division of planting lands. In the Old Town Records of 3 March 1649, Mr. (i.e. Gentry) and two other town members (Howes and Thacher) were accused of making unequal transactions of lands at Mattachusett. The committee was thus deterred from bringing more people into the area without the Governor's agreement. Mr. Croe was also accused of having more property than his due. John had acquired 100 acres of upland and 20 acres of meadow.

These allegations did not deter Croe from being an important member of the community. From 1640-1643 he was a magistrate in the lower court, on those cases not exceeding a fine of 20 shillings.

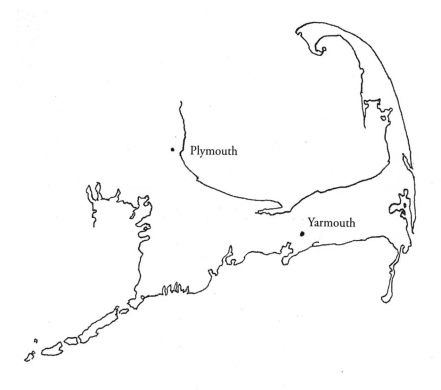

Pioneers of Billerica • Settling the Shawshine Wilderness: 1654-1660

John and his wife Elishua had a large two-story home at Yarmouth that was called a palisade house, i.e. it was a block house for defense against Indians and possibly pirates that roamed the surrounding waters. The lower floor was constructed of stone and the upper floor of timber. Shell mortar held it together for over 200 years.

John Croe died at Yarmouth 7 January 1672. He was about 82 years old. Elishua survived him until 1688. He did not leave a will.

Pioneers of Billerica • Settling the Shawshine Wilderness: 1654-1660

Founding Father

SIMON CROSBY

Son of Simon Crosby and Ann (Brigham) Crosby

m. (1) ----, Rachel Bracket, daughter of Richard & Allis (Blower) Bracket
and sister to Mary, Peter and John Bracket
b. 3 Nov. 1639, Boston, MA
d. 1735, Billerica, MA

Children	Born	Married	Died
1. Rachel	20 Aug. 1660, Billerica, MA	1685, Ephraim Kidder	14 Sept. 1721, Billerica, MA
2. Simon	1663, Billerica, MA	(1) Before 1689, Hannah Everett	22 Jan. 1725, Billerica, MA
		(2) 1702, Abigail Parker	
3. Thomas	10 Mar. 1665/6, Billerica, MA	----	1725-1737 Billerica, MA
4. Joseph	5 Jul. 1665, Billerica, MA	1691, Sarah French	----, Billerica, MA
5. Hannah	30 Mar. 1672, Billerica, MA	(1) 1694/5, Samuel Danforth	3 Oct. 1752, Billerica, MA
		(2) 1743, Enoch Kidder	
6. Nathan	9 Feb. 1674/5, Billerica, MA	1706, Sarah Shed	11 Apr. 1749, Billerica, MA
7. Josiah	11 Nov. 1677, Billerica, MA	1703, Mary Manning	Oct. 1745, Billerica, MA
8. Mary	23 Nov. 1680, Billerica, MA	1701, John Blanchard	7 May 1748, Billerica, MA
9. Sarah	27 July 1684, Billerica, MA	1706, William Rawson	After 1733, Braintree, MA

Simon Crosby

b.	*August 1637, Cambridge, MA*
m.	*15 July 1659, Rachel Bracket, --------*
d.	*22 January 1725/6, Billerica, MA*

Simon's parents: Ann (Brigham) and Simon Crosby emigrated to Cambridge, MA in April 1635 on the ship "Susan and Ellen" with their first son Thomas, then eight weeks old. They had made the journey from Yorkshire in northeast England to come to America.

When young Simon was 14 years old, his father died, age 31, leaving Ann, three sons and property in Cambridge and Rowley, MA. In October 1651, his mother, now remarried as Anna Thompson, wanted to settle the estate for the children {MA Archives Vol. 15B:180a, 181-2]. The Crosbys had many material possessions, animals, grain, a new frame house and barns and seven acres of land in Cambridge. The real estate value was set at £140.0.0. Simon, Jr. was to have £5 at the age of 21.

In 1659, Simon Crosby married Rachel Bracket, the sister of Mary, John and Peter Bracket, founding fathers. The couple moved to Billerica and encouraged her siblings to also make their home in the fine new developing region. Simon built a log cabin in 1660 on the north side of Bare Hill on the Bedford Road. With the legacy from his father and funds gained from his own employment, his cabin became the wing of a large two-story house.

Between 1672 and 1686, he ran a house of public entertainment. This inn was a source of food and drink, the post office, and a local gathering place for gossip, politicking and revelry. Perhaps he thought of another form of employment, because he sold the inn in 1686. However, two years later, he reopened a hostelry for wayfarers and the house of public entertainment.

He was probably the town's first landlord and was a well-known citizen of the area. During the anxieties of Indian tension in 1675/6, his home served as a garrison for nine men and seven families. Between the years 1690 and 1698, he was a constable and deputy to the Massachusetts General Court.

of Compound Sallet

Your Compound Sallets,
are first the young buds and knots of all manner of Wholesome
Herbs at their first springing; as red Sage, Mint, Lettuce,
Violets, Marigolds, Spinage, and many others mixed together,
and then served up to the Table with Vinegar,
Sallet-Oyl, and Sugar.

Gervaise Markham, ca. 1615

A Sixteenth Century Salad for 6 persons

12 spinach leaves
6 Cabbage leaves, shredded
two sliced lettuce hearts
6 dill pickles slides
12 green olives
2 tablespoons capers
1/2 cup raisins or currants
24 blanched almonds slides in half and
  browned in butter
4 dried figs, chopped

Dressing
3 parts olive oil
1 part vinegar
sugar
salt and pepper
1/2 teaspoon hot mustard

before serving, decorate with violtes, borage leaves, or
marsh marigolds, rosemary, or elder, nasturtium

As it appeared at the turn of the century, the home of Simon Crosby.

Simon Crosby died 22 January 1725/6 in Billerica, having written a lengthy will [Middlesex Probate #5369] in 1724. It was difficult to read as well as torn and mended. He wanted his wife Rachel to have use of the estate and was most generous in bequeathing her £6 annually for the rest of her life. The eldest son Simon had already received his benefit and the four other sons: Thomas, Joseph, Nathan and Josiah, were each to have £80 and the four daughters: Rachel, Hannah, Mary and Sarah, each £60.

Founding Father

JONATHAN DANFORTH
The youngest son of Nicholas and Elizabeth (Barber) Danforth
m.   (1)   22 Nov. 1654, Elizabeth Poulter, Boston, MA
        b. 1 Sept. 1633, Raleigh, Essex, England
        Daughter of John and Mary Poulter. Sister of John Poulter, founding father.
        d. 7 Oct. 1689, ——

Children	Born	Married	Died
1. Mary	27 Jan. 1655/6, Billerica, MA	1678, John Parker	After 1713, Chelmsford, MA
2. Elizabeth	27 May 1657, Billerica, MA	1687, Simon Heywood (Hayward)	After 1713, Concord, MA
3. Jonathan	18 Feb. 1658/9, Billerica, MA Harvard graduate	1682, Rebecca Parker	17 Jan. 1710/11, Billerica, MA
4. John	23 Jan. 1660/1, Billerica, MA	--------	died young
5. John	22 Feb. 1661/2, Billerica, MA	--------	died young
6. Lydia	1 June 1664, ———	———, Edward Wright	After 1725, Concord, MA
7. Samuel	5 Feb. 1665/6, Billerica, MA	1694/5, Hannah Crosby	19 Apr. 1742, Billerica, MA
8. Anna	8 Mar. 1667/8, Billerica, MA	1689/90, Oliver Whiting	13 Aug. 1737, Billerica, MA
9. Thomas	29 April 1670, Billerica, MA	--------	31 July 1670, Billerica, MA
10. Nicholas	1 July 1671, Billerica, MA		8 Mar. 1693/4, Billerica, MA
11. Sarah	23 Dec. 1676, Billerica, MA	(1) 1695, William French	1729, Concord, MA
		(2) 1729, Ebenezer Davis	

Jonathan Danforth ★

Jonathan Danforth

b.	*29 February 1628, Framlingham, Suffolk, England*
emig.	*1635*
m.	*(1) 22 November 1654, Elizabeth Poulter, Boston, MA*
	(2) 17 November 1690, Esther (Champney) Converse, Billerica, MA
	7 September 1712, Billerica, MA

Jonathan Danforth has been called the father of the town of Billerica, MA. An energetic, educated man, he took on responsibilities avidly and skillfully. He was a primary surveyor in the town, but also in adjoining communities including Groton, Dunstable and Dracut and as far as Litchfield, NH. He was the town clerk for 21 years (1665-1686) keeping the vital records up to date and legible, land grants descriptive and established in the archives. Jonathan kept a close eye on protecting the town with fortifications and ammunition.

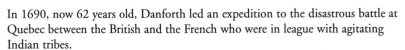

The Danforth Home, which stood West of Boston Road.

He was Captain of the Billerica Militia for a number of years, and in 1675, took his troops to Quabog Pond, Brookfield, MA in an Indian battle where Timothy Farley was killed and John French wounded.

In 1690, now 62 years old, Danforth led an expedition to the disastrous battle at Quebec between the British and the French who were in league with agitating Indian tribes.

Jonathan was one of the 14 signers of the Shawshine settlers petition to be a separate township from Cambridge, MA in 1654/5. He was part of the committee for setting up farm and house lots in the town. His home, later a well-known garrison was built at River Street and Boston Road in the center of the village.

Pioneers of Billerica • Settling the Shawshine Wilderness: 1654-1660

Founding Father

JONATHAN DANFORTH

m. (2) 17 Nov. 1690, Esther (Champney) Converse, Billerica, MA

bp. 31 Oct. 1630, Stisted, England
Daughter of Elder Richard Champney, founding father.
Widow of Josiah Converse of Woburn, MA.
d. 5 Apr. 1713, Billerica, MA

Children	Born	Married	Died

Pioneers of Billerica • Settling the Shawshine Wilderness: 1654-1660

Jonathan Danforth was born in Framlingham, Suffolk, England 9 February 1628 to Elizabeth (Barber) and Nicholas Danforth. The family emigrated to Cambridge, MA in 1635 where his father, an educated man, was an innkeeper, licensed to sell liquor. Nicholas acquired considerable property at Newtown and Cambridge, and was active in town politics and on committees setting out property lines.

Jonathan married twice. His first wife and mother of his 11 children was Elizabeth Poulter, the sister of John Poulter, another founding father. Elizabeth had also been born in England and had been willed £100 by her father when she was 21 years old (1654). It is most likely that her estate contributed to the move to Billerica.

The couple's children were born in Billerica between 1655/6 and 1676. Elizabeth died 7 October 1689. About a year later, on 17 November 1690, Jonathan married Esther Champney Converse, the daughter of Elder Richard Champney and the widow of Josiah Converse.

Jonathan Danforth died 7 September 1712 and Esther 7 months later 5 April 1713 in Billerica [Mdsx. Pro. #5891].

Jonathan's will of 1709 was noteworthy for the attention to detail in his enumeration of gifts and his evaluation of his real estate as already bestowed on his children. He and his wife Esther had retired to a small section of the homestead, where he expected Esther would continue to live in her widowhood. He willed her £4 a year as his widow, and gave her a gift of £5. However, if she remarried, she would benefit by only 40 shillings a year.

The remainder of the estate was to be divided equally with his seven children. Although Jonathan, Jr., as the oldest son, was to have a double portion. His granddaughter Mary Parker "that lives with me" was to have £5, plus the prior gifts of a featherbed and furniture. His grandson Samuel Danforth "that lives with me" had already been given gifts, but if he continues "in my servis" until 21 year of age, he was to have £30.

The executors chosen were sons Jonathan and Samuel Danforth and son-in-law Oliver Whiting.

In the inventory of his estate which listed his land holdings with a value of £461, were included other evaluations and charges. It appears that Jonathan Danforth's funeral was a special one for the charges were noted to be £20.12.04. In addition, following this ceremony was an additional charge of £8 for cider and provisions.

Danforth's oldest son Jonathan died before his father in 1710/1. Following the deaths of Esther and Jonathan, Sr., the executors sold the homestead and the pasture of 10 acres, valued at £200. Jonathan, Jr.'s heirs benefited, and the remainder was equally divided among the six other children.

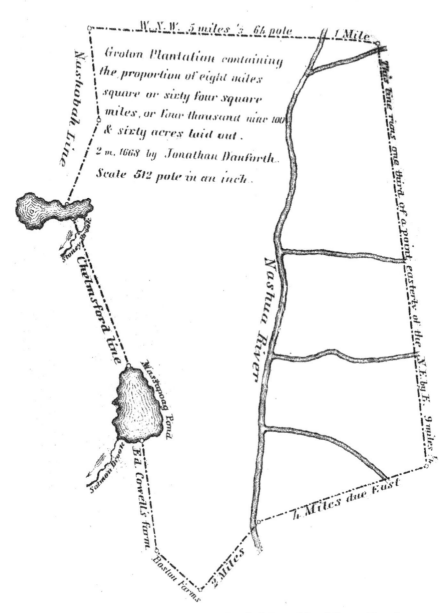

A Danforth Survey Map of Groton, Massachusetts

Pioneers of Billerica • Settling the Shawshine Wilderness: 1654-1660

Founding Father

JOHN DURRANT

m.   16 Nov. 1670, Susan Dutton of Woburn, MA

b. 27 Dec. 1653, --------

Daughter of Thomas Dutton, Sr. and Susannah (Palmer) Dutton

d. ------

Children	Born	Married	Died
1. John	31 July 1672, Billerica, MA	1695, Elizabeth Jaquith	25 Feb. 1757, Billerica, MA
2. Thomas	7 Jan. 1674/5, Billerica, MA	1702, Sara Jaquith	-----
3. Abigail	24 Sept. 1681, Billerica, MA	1697, Abraham Ireland	-----
4. Mehitable	20 Apr. 1687, Billerica, MA	-----	-----

Pioneers of Billerica • Settling the Shawshine Wilderness: 1654-1660

John Durrant

b.	*@1645, Lynn, MA*
m.	*16 November 1670, Susan Dutton, Billerica, MA*
d.	*27 October 1692, Cambridge, MA*

In November 1659 when a lad, John Durrant acquired a house lot of 20 acres north of the village of Billerica, MA west of the Boston Road, near the Concord River, beyond Abbott's Bridge. He was most likely a farmer in the good weather seasons and a hunter, woodsman and laborer in the winter months. Money seems to have been tight for his family required financial aid from the town in 1676 and 1677 as recorded in the Billerica Town Record.

John was born @1645 in Lynn, MA and married Susan Dutton 16 November 1670 in Billerica. They had four children in this town, two sons marrying into the Jaquith family.

John died in prison in Cambridge, MA 27 October 1692, presumably with charges relating to the Salem witchcraft trials. No record of this charge has been located.

His widow Susan married Justinian Holden in 1693. They lived a short time in Billerica, but in 1695, when Justinian had problems with the tax collectors, the family moved to Holden, MA beyond Wachusett Reservoir.

Founding Father

GEORGE FARLEY

Son of Thomas Farley and Jane Hungerford

   m.   Christian Births

       b. ——

          In 1639, she emigrated from Sweden with her father and sister Hannah.

          Her father died on the crossing.

       d. ——

Children	Born	Married	Died
1. James	23 Nov. 1643, ———	Unmarried	10 Dec. 1643, ———
2. Caleb	1 Apr. 1645, Woburn, MA	(1) 1666, Rebecca Hill	16 Mar. 1711, Billerica, MA
		(2) 1669, Lydia More	
3. Mary	27 Feb. 1646/7, ———	——, John Sanders	31 Aug. 1712, Billerica, MA
4. Samuel	Last week Mar. 1654, Billerica, MA	1677, Elizabeth Shed	———
5. Mehitabell	Last week April 1656, Billerica, MA		1 Feb. 1672/3, Billerica, MA
6. Timothy	——, Woburn, MA	———	2 Aug. 1675, Brookfield, MA
			Killed by Indians
7. Elizabeth	———	———	

Pioneers of Billerica • Settling the Shawshine Wilderness: 1654-1660

George Farley

b.	*1615 Bristol, Somersetshire, England*
emig.	*1639 on the ship "Lion"*
m.	*9 April 1641, Christian Births, Woburn, MA*
d.	*23 November 1693, Billerica, MA*

As early as 1653/4 George Farley moved into the Shawshine Tract from Charlestown and Woburn, MA. He had come to the Massachusetts Bay Colony in 1639 on the ship "Lion," a Baptist in search of greater religious freedom and opportunity to acquire land for farming and his clothier's business.

George bought the northwest lot on the Dudley Farm, and built his family home at Bedford and Charnstaffe Roads. He was one of the signers of the General Court Shawshine-Cambridge Agreement in February 1654.

Farley was born in 1615 in Farleigh, Bristol, Somersetshire, England. His Farleigh ancestors had lived in Somersetshire since William the Conqueror granted land to them. In the 17th century, another relative Sir Thomas Hungerford and his son Walter built the castle from an existing manor.

George married Christian Births 9 April 1641 in Woburn. She had emigrated to America in 1639 with her father and (probable) sister Hannah. Mr. Births died during the crossing.

In 1675 at the height of the Indian anxieties, the family's house was used as a garrison in "time of extremity."

George and Christian had seven children. Tragically, their son Timothy was killed at Quahog Pond, Brookfield, MA 2 August 1675 during King Philip's War.

George's faith may have been tested more than once for on 18 June 1672 he did not go to the daylong church service. This day was soon after their daughter Mehittabell, age 16, had died. George was fined by the community religious people for non-attendance at church.

Pioneers of Billerica • Settling the Shawshine Wilderness: 1654-1660

He died on 23 November 1693 in Billerica, age 78, with three of his seven children in the community. Christian died 27 March 1702.

SAM^ᵘˡ and NATH^ᵘᵐ BucK

Pioneers of Billerica • Settling the Shawshine Wilderness: 1654-1660

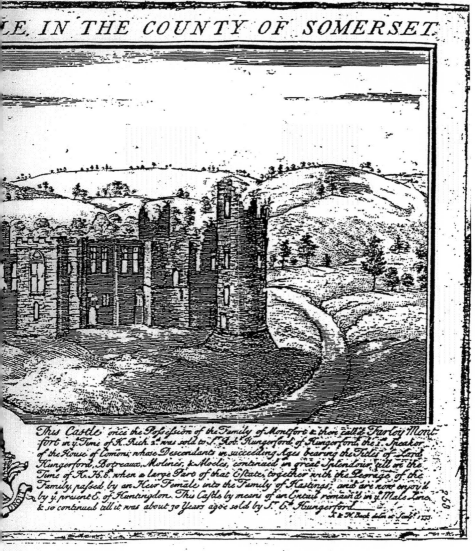

LE, IN THE COUNTY OF SOMERSET.

This Castle once the Possession of the Family of Montfort & then call'd Farley Mont
fort in y. Time of K. Rich. 2. was sold to S. Rob. Hungerford of Hungerford the 1. Speaker
of the House of Comons whose Descendants in succeeding Ages bearing the Titles of Lord
Hungerford, Botreaux, Molines, & Moeles, continued in great Splendour till in the
Time of K. H. 8. when a large Part of that Estate, together with the Peerage of the
Family, passed by an Heir Female into the Family of Hastings; and are now enjoy'd
by y present E. of Huntingdon. This Castle by means of an Entail remain'd in y Male Line
& so continued till it was about 30 Years agoe sold by S. E. Hungerford.

CASTLE   Del.t et Sculp.t 1733 A.D.

Pioneers of Billerica • Settling the Shawshine Wilderness: 1654-1660

THOMAS FOSTER

m. ——, Elizabeth ——
b. ——
d. ——

Children	Born	Married	Died
1. Thomas	18 Aug. 1640, Weymouth, MA	——, Sarah Parker	16 Sept. 1679, Cambridge, MA
	A doctor	Sarah's second husband was Peter Bracket, a founding father	
2. Sarah	-----	1662, Samuel Kemp, founding father	——, Groton, MA
3. John	7 Oct. 1642, Weymouth, MA	(1) 1663, Mary Chillingsworth	13 June 1732, Marshfield, MA
	A blacksmith	(2) 1702, Sarah Thomas	
4. Elizabeth	-----	1666/7, James Frost	1726, Billerica, MA
		A deacon	
5. Experience	-----	1663, Joseph French	-----
6. Increase			
7. Hopestill	26 Mar. 1648, Braintree, MA	1670, Elizabeth (Pierce) Whittemore	26 May 1679, Woburn, MA
	A blacksmith		
8. Joseph	28 Mar. 1650, Braintree, MA	(1) 1672, Alice Gorton	4 Dec. 1721, Billerica, MA
		(2) ——, Margaret Brown	
		(3) ——, Rebecca Danforth	
		Widow of Jonathan Danforth	
9. Jonathan	-----	1692, Abigail Kimball	——, Boxford, MA
	A blacksmith		

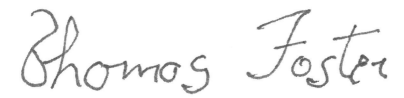

Thomas Foster

b.	*@162-, England*
emig.	*before 1640*
m.	*@1638, Elizabeth --------, probably in England, possibly Weymouth, MA*
d.	*20 April 1682, Billerica, MA*

The first birth records located for Thomas Foster's two sons Thomas and John were in Weymouth, MA in 1640 and 1642. The Fosters did not settle in Weymouth, but moved to the more cohesive religious community of Braintree, MA.

Weymouth (previously called Wessagusset) had had a very perilous beginning with one of the London Adventurers: Mr. Thomas Weston. The Adventurers had been financially behind the settlement at Plymouth, MA and the sailing of the Mayflower, but Weston himself was not reliable in fulfilling his promises and did not shy away from illegal schemes. The new town had many difficulties with Indians, as well as the more puritanical Plymouth Colony. In spite of this, Weymouth has been recognized as the second oldest English community in New England (1627).

Thomas Foster and his growing family were in Braintree before 26 March 1648. At least three more of his nine children were born there.

Foster was made a Freeman in 1657, attesting to his good religious and community record. He was a blacksmith, a trade which he taught to his sons. Three of his sons chose blacksmithing as their occupation, but the oldest son became a doctor in Roxbury, MA.

In June 1659, Thomas was granted a home lot of 50 acres at the east end of Bare Hill, Billerica. It was close to Webb's Brook, at the intersection of Boston Road and Wyman.

Foster immediately became a valuable member to the community for his blacksmithing skills, but he was also a selectman 1659-1669. In 1660, he was chosen the eldest Corporal of the "Trayne Band", the Billerica militia. Thomas appears to have been a practical person, who was willing to accept coal for his occupational use that was not usable at the forge in Braintree. He was given about 2.5 loads of coal.

In November 1670, Thomas Richardson, a three year resident of Billerica and tenant of the Church Farm, was charged with taking two loads of cedar out of the town woods and given a fine of 30 shillings. Thomas Foster paid this fine, and Richardson returned the favor by agreeing to build Foster 22 poles of four-rail fence (about 50 feet).

On 18 June 1672, Foster was fined along with some other community members for not attending church, an all-day affair. However, this was a repeat offence for him and was punished by the Middlesex County Court in 1671 and 1675. However, he was forgiven by the church enough to be made a deacon.

One senses that Thomas must have had some doubts about his and the church's convictions, for he became involved with the Anabaptists (Baptist Church) on the Lord's Day. For this offense, he was fined £5.8.6.

Foster married Elizabeth --------, perhaps in England or in Weymouth. She outlived him, dying 29 January 1694/5 in Billerica, MA.

Thomas Foster died 20 April 1682, and bequeathed his wife Elizabeth furnishings and the use of the home to be "comfortable" the rest of her life. His son-in-law James Frost (husband of daughter Elizabeth) was to have a good cow. His son Joseph Foster was the executor of the estate of £98.17.0. Perhaps Thomas gave money or property to his children during his lifetime [will Middlesex Co. #8272B].

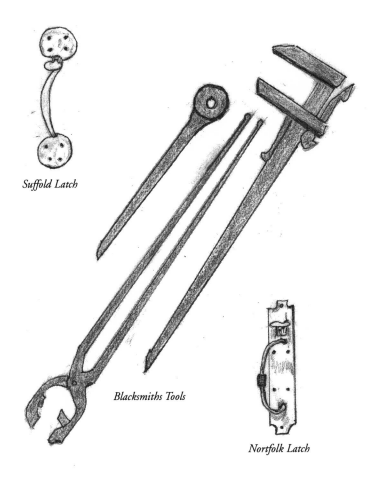

Suffold Latch

Blacksmiths Tools

Nortfolk Latch

Founding Father

JOHN FRENCH

Son of Elizabeth and William French, founding father

m. (1) ------, Abigail Coggin, ------

b. c.1637, Barnstable, MA

d. 5 Apr. 1662, Billerica, MA

Children	Born	Married	Died

Pioneers of Billerica • Settling the Shawshine Wilderness: 1654-1660

John French

b.	*1635, Halstead, Suffolk County, England*
emig.	*1635 on the ship "Defence"*
m.	*(1) 21 June 1659, Abigail Coggin, Barnstable, MA*
	(2) 3 July 1662, Hannah Burrage, --------
	(3) 14 January 1667/8, Mary Rogers, Billerica, MA
	(4) 16 January 1677/8, Mary (Littlefield) Kitterige, Billerica, MA
d.	*October 1712, Billerica, MA*

William French, Esquire, one of the founding fathers of Billerica, MA had four sons: Francis, John, Jacob and Samuel. Francis seems to have died early and Samuel died in 1646. John and Jacob both made their homes in Billerica, John in 1654 and Jacob some years later. Along with his father, John French is one of Billerica's founding fathers. Born in England, he was an infant when the family arrived in Cambridge, MA. He grew up with this socially prominent, well-do-do family where education was valued.

John acquired property on the south side of Fox Hill, south of Allen Street, in an area called Loes Plain.

French was active in community service, and during King Philip's War in 1675, was in the militia as a corporal. He was severely wounded in the fighting of the disastrous battle at Quabog, near Brookfield, MA. Soon after this injury, he appealed for relief from Billerica, stating he was a "poor wounded man" [Hazen GR, p. 56].

John French married four times.

His first wife was Abigail Coggin, whom he married 21 June 1659. She was the daughter of Abigail (Bishop) and Henry Coggin of Barnstable, MA. Her father was a sea captain between London and Boston, who had a financial investment with his brother John Coggin in more than one of the voyages. Abigail died 5 April 1662 in Billerica.

On 3 July 1662, French married Hannah Burrage, the daughter of John Burrage of Charlestown, MA. The couple had two daughters: Hannah and Abigail. This second wife died 7 July 1667 in Billerica.

Founding Father

JOHN FRENCH

m. (2) ——, Hannah Burridge, ——
b. 1643, ——
Daughter of John Burridge of Charlestown, MA
d. 7 July 1667, Billerica, MA

Children	Born	Married	Died
1. Hannah	20 Jan. 1663/4, Billerica, MA	1685, John Kittredge	27 Mar. 1689/90, Billerica, MA
2. Abigail	6 Dec. 1665, Billerica, MA	1697, Benjamin Parker	13 Mar. 1722/3, Billerica, MA

Pioneers of Billerica • Settling the Shawshine Wilderness: 1654-1660

In needing a mother for his two children, John married 14 January 1668 Mary Rogers, the daughter of Priscilla (Dawes) and John Rogers, one of the founding families in Billerica. Mary and John had one daughter named Mary. John's third wife Mary died 6 June 1677 in Billerica.

French's fourth wife was Mary (Littlefield) Kitterige, the widow of founding father John Kitterige (Kittredge). They were married 16 January 1677/8. Mary Kitterige was the daughter of Francis Littlefield from Woburn, MA. The Kitterige's had had five sons, b. 1665-1677, so when John and Mary had three sons and three daughters, many of the older children of both marriages were adults before the youngest were born, between 1679 and 1692/3.

John French died October 1712 in Billerica at age 77, intestate. On 27 October 1712, an article of agreement [#8495] was drawn up between the heirs. The eldest son John had received his full portion by deed from his father before John, Sr.'s death. The remaining heirs concluded that the estate could not be divided among them without damage to the estate of land, house and movables. Thus, it was decided, the second son William was to have all the lands and house. Mary French, John's widow, was to have use of the living room and bed chamber in the west end of the house. She was to have adequate furnishings and room in the cellar for, on a yearly basis: 12 bushels of Indian meal, four bushels of rye meal, 150 pounds of pork, firewood, 15 pounds of flax, wool and a cow.

In exchange for the property, William French gave to his siblings the following: "Brother" Thomas Abbot married to Elizabeth French £12, Benjamin Parker married to Abigail French £17, Nathan Shed married to Mary French £11, Joseph Frost married to Sarah French £12, John Kitterige married to Hannah French b. 1663/4 £11, and another daughter Hannah French b. 1692/3, still single, to have £20.

Mary French, John French's widow died 17 October 1719.

Pioneers of Billerica • Settling the Shawshine Wilderness: 1654-1660

Founding Father

JOHN FRENCH

m. (3) ------, Mary Rogers, ------
      b. 26 Oct. 1643, Watertown, MA
         Daughter of Priscilla (Dawes) & John Rogers, a founding father
      d. 16 June 1677, Billerica, MA

Children	Born	Married	Died
3. Mary	4 Mar. 1669/70, Billerica, MA	1693/4, Nathan Shed	21 Aug.1740, Billerica, MA

Pioneers of Billerica • Settling the Shawshine Wilderness: 1654-1660

Founding Father

JOHN FRENCH

m. (4) ――――, Mary (Littlefield) Kittredge, ――――
Daughter of Francis Littlefield. Widow of John Kittredge, founding father.
b. 14 Dec. 1646, Woburn, MA
d. 17 Oct. 1719, Billerica, MA

Children	Born	Married	Died
4. John	15 May, 1679, Billerica, MA	1707/8, Ruth Richardson	Before 1712, ――――
5. Elizabeth	24 July 1681, Billerica, MA	1706, Thomas Abbott	After 1712, ――――
6. William	26 Nov. 1683, Billerica, MA	――――	21 Apr. 1685, Billerica, MA
7. Sarah	15 Sept. 1685, Billerica, MA	(1) ――――, George Flint	1717/8, ――――
		(2) 1710, Joseph Frost	
8. William	8 Aug. 1687, Billerica, MA	――――, Mehitable Patten	25 Feb. 1745/6, ――――
9. Hannah	18 Feb.1692/3, Billerica, MA	(1) 1713, Jonathan Richardson	12 Sept. 1769, Billerica, MA
		(2) 1725/6, Benjamin Frost	

Pioneers of Billerica • Settling the Shawshine Wilderness: 1654-1660

Founding Father
WILLIAM FRENCH

m. (1) c.1625, Elizabeth ?Godfrey/Symes, England
b. 1603-1607, England
d. 31 Mar. 1668, Billerica, MA

Children	Born	Married	Died
1. Francis	1625, England	---------	After 1635, ---------
2. Elizabeth	1629, England	1650, Richard Ellis	---------
3. Mary	1632, England	----, Jonathan Hide	---------
4. John	1635, England	(1) 1659, Abigail Coggan	Oct. 1712, Billerica, MA
	bp. Sept. 1635, Cambridge, MA	(2) 1667, Hannah Burrage	
		(3) 1668, Mary Rogers	
		(4) 1688, Mary L. Kittredge	
5. Sarah	Mar. 1638, Cambridge, MA	1660, Jonathan Peake	1694, Roxbury, MA
6. Jacob	16 Jan. 1639, Cambridge, MA	(1) 1665, Mary Champney	20 May 1713, Billerica, Ma
		(2) 1685, Mary Converse	
		(3) ----, Mary ---------	
7. Hannah	2 Feb. 1641, Cambridge, MA	---------	30 June 1642, Cambridge, MA
8. Hannah	16 Feb. 1644, Cambridge, MA	1661, John Bracket	9 May 1674, Billerica, MA
		A founding father	
9. Samuel	3 Dec. 1645, Cambridge, MA		15 July 1646, Billerica, MA

Note: bp. 5 Sept. 1636, Cambridge, MA (appears under Born for Elizabeth/Mary area)

Pioneers of Billerica • Settling the Shawshine Wilderness: 1654-1660

William French, Captain

b.	*15 March 1603, Halstead, Suffolk County, England*
emig.	*1635 on the ship "Defence"*
m.	*(1) @1625 Elizabeth ?Godfrey/Symes, England*
	(2) 6 May 1669, Mary (Lathrop) Sternes, Billerica, MA
d.	*20 November 1681, Billerica, MA*

William French was 49 years old when he and his wife Elizabeth and five children came to Billerica from Cambridge, MA. He had resided in that town about 17 years and became a Freeman there in 1635/6.

In February 1635, William had owned 150 acres in Cambridge, as noted in the listing of houses in that town.

In his quest for more land, French was a very early purchaser of Shawshine property in 1652, buying lot #24 of 150 acres. He was one of the negotiators of the Shawshine Settlement to become separate from Cambridge, MA and be known as Billerica. William acquired part of the Dudley Farm at Indian Hill, northeast of Nutting Pond, a 20-acre lot or 226 acres of upland and 24 acres of meadow. His house was situated near the "turnpike," i.e. east of Concord Road.

When William French was 30 years old, he sailed to Massachusetts on the "Defence" with his wife Eliza, age 32. With them were four of their children: Francis 10, Elizabeth 6, Marie 2, and John 5 months. The couple were servants to a young English couple Roger and Eliza Harlakenden along with his sister Mabe. William had acquired some education and was a tailor by trade.

Before leaving Cambridge, William had acquired military service as a Lieutenant 1642-1647, and after moving to Billerica, he continued to be involved in military affairs as a Captain.

Between 1660 and 1664, French was a deputy from Billerica to the Massachusetts Bay General Court. He was a justice of the peace in 1667, and frequently solemnized marriages.

Pioneers of Billerica • Settling the Shawshine Wilderness: 1654-1660

Founding Father
WILLIAM FRENCH

m. (2) ——, Mary (Lathrop) Sternes, ——

b. 4 Oct. 1640, Barnstable, MA; daughter of Mary (Learned) and Thomas Lathrop.

First husband: John Sternes (founding father); she married Isaac Mixer 29 June 1687.

d. After 1735, Watertown, MA

Children	Born	Married	Died
10. Mary	3 Apr. 1670, Billerica, MA	(1) 1687, Robert Sharp	?1695/6, Woburn, MA
		(2) 1693/4, Nathaniel Dunckler	
11. Sarah	28 Oct. 1671, Billerica, MA	1691, Joseph Crosby	——, Billerica, MA
12. Abigail	14 Apr. 1673, Billerica, MA		13 Apr. 1674, Billerica, MA
13. Hannah	25 Jan. 1676, Billerica, MA	1693, John Child	1766, ——
William and Elizabeth French named two of their daughters: Mary (b. 1632) and Hannah (b. 1644).			
William and Mary French named two of their daughters: Mary (b. 1670) and Hannah (b. 1676).			

Pioneers of Billerica • *Settling the Shawshine Wilderness: 1654-1660*

The French Garrison, scene of an Indian Attack in 1675.

William's wife Eliza, mother of nine of his children, died in Billerica 31 March 1668. French married for the second time to Mary (Lathrop) Sternes, the widow of founding father Lt. John Sternes of Billerica. She had five children when they married 6 May 1669.

William and Mary's marriage lasted 12 years, blessed by four children. The youngest child Hannah, born in 1676, was five years old when her father died in Billerica 20 Nov. 1681. French's widow Mary married for the third time 29 June 1687 to Isaac Mixer of Watertown, MA. The three youngest surviving French girls were unmarried at that time: Mary, Sarah and Hannah.

William French left a will in Middlesex Co. [#8528], but was of such poor legibility, the content could not be read.

Mary (Lathrop/Sternes/French) Mixer deeded to her son Samuel Sternes of Billerica March 1702 four acres and 20 poles, part of the estate of her late husband John Sternes [BK. 10 p. 525]. Samuel was obligated not to sell this land, unless to his brothers, without her consent.

Mary (Lathrop/Sternes/French) Mixer died after 1735 in Watertown.

Founding Father
WILLIAM HAILE

m. (1) ----, Anna Case, Charlestown, MA
  b. ----
  Her second husband was Samuel Trull
  d. 1692, --------

Children	Born	Married	Died
None			

Pioneers of Billerica • Settling the Shawshine Wilderness: 1654-1660

William Haile

b.   -----
m.   *30 October 1662, Anna Case, Charlestown, MA*
d.   *20 May 1668, Billerica, MA*

William Haile was granted one quarter of a 10-acre lot in 1659, which would have been 30+ acres, and a home lot 24 acres on the east side of the Concord River, on the west side of the Boston Road, just below the "Great Bridge" crossing the Concord River in North Billerica, MA.

William was the first person employed in town to "digg ye graves" [Hazen, GR, p.65]. He also did some weaving as noted in an inventory of his belongings after his death.

In 1661, he signed the Parker Agreement stating that John Parker and Jonathan Danforth were each to have 1,000 acres of a 4,000-grant the General Court had allowed Billerica. The remaining acres were to be laid out for others to have in the town.

In 1664, Haile signed an Oath of Allegiance to the King of England.

William married Anna Case 30 October 1662 in Charlestown, MA. They had no children. William died 20 May 1668 in Billerica. An inventory was taken of his estate 1 June 1668 [Middlesex probate 3:36-7]. He had few clothes, but did have a chest, a "snapsacke" sword and Pike. He had 15 pounds of yarn that was dressed, flax and cotton wool, bags and hops, a wooden wheel, a linen winding wheel and Indian corn. Included in the list were two smoothing irons and a gridiron for cooking food. He also had acquired 20 acres of land and a house.

On 15 June 1668 Anna married Samuel Trull, who was a Billerica resident with a small parcel of land and a cow or two. Samuel and Anna had a 24 year marriage before her death in 1692.

Probably after she died, Trull was not able to manage very well and became a ward of Billerica. In 1701, the town built a log home for him that measured 18 by 24 feet. Samuel Trull died 17 May 1714 in Billerica with the town paying for his burial.

Founding Father
WILLIAM HAMLET

m.   ------, Sarah (?Ives) Hubbard
     b. c.1598, England
        Widow of James Hubbard
     d. 18 Jan. 1689, Woburn, MA

Children	Born	Married	Died
1. Rebecca	bp. 16--, Cambridge, MA	1664, James Frost	20 July 1666, Billerica, MA
2. Jacob	bp. 1641, Cambridge, MA	(1) 1668, Hannah Parker	1703, Woburn, MA
		(2) 1669, Mary Dutton	
		(3) ------, Mary Jacquith	
Sarah had with first husband, James Hubbard:			
Thomas	10 Aug. 1638, --------	------, Elizabeth Huitt	------

Pioneers of Billerica • Settling the Shawshine Wilderness: 1654-1660

William Hamlet

b.   *@1614, England*
emig.   -----
m.   -----, *Sarah (Ives) Hubbard,* --------
d.   *after 1679, Woburn, MA*

William Hamlet, his wife Sarah and their two youths: Jacob and Rebecca arrived in Billerica in 1656. When first married, William and Sarah had a home in Watertown, MA for the years 1642-5. He purchased some land in Charlestown, MA, which he then resold to move to Cambridge, MA where he became a Freeman in 1651. In 1652, Cambridge allotted him 60 acres of land.

Hamlet was a carpenter in Cambridge, where the town gave him permission to down three trees and two "clapboard" trees for his employment, but "not out of town" [Cambridge Town Records]. In 1650, William was chosen with others to look after the Cow Common and to be sure that no cattle roamed free.

It is significant that Hamlet's personality was noted in this commentary in the Cambridge Town Records [p. 115]: "The Townfesmen do agree and confent that Ed: Goffe, Ri: Jacfon and Thomas Danforth or any of them fhall fett out to William Hamlett, fo much of the Rocks annent his houfe, as they shall find him to damnified by the highway crofsing his land."

In 1656, perhaps for reasons related to more suitable land, opportunity for employment, or perhaps due to religious convictions, the Hamlets moved to Billerica. William was a staunch Baptist, who upheld his belief in adult, not infant, baptism. Billerica gave him 125 acres of land on Bare Hill: 113 acres of upland and 12 acres of meadow with all town privileges. This property was on the northeast corner of the hill between Boston Road and Webb's Brook.

In 1679, when William and Sarah were elderly, they exchanged their property with Caleb Farley of Woburn, MA who was also Baptist. William died sometime after this date, and Sarah died 18 January 1689 in Woburn. William Hamlet did not leave a will.

Founding Father
RALPH HILL, JR.

m. ——, Martha Toothaker, ——
b. c.1636, either Plymouth or Woburn, MA
Daughter of Margaret (——) and Roger Toothaker, Sr.
d. 4 Jan. 1703/4, Billerica, MA

Children	Born	Married	Died
1. Elizabeth	28 July 1661, Billerica, MA	1687, Timothy Baldwin	26 Jan. 1703/4, ——
2. Deborah	14 Dec. 1663, Billerica, MA	1690, John Sheldon	11 Jan 1730, Billerica, MA
3. Rebecca	14 Aug. 1666, Billerica, MA	——	Before 1695, Billerica, MA
4. Samuel	18 Feb. 1671/2, Billerica, MA	——, Deborah ——	4 Aug. 1756, Billerica, MA
	A Captain		After father's death 1695, Billerica, MA
5. Daniel	22 Feb. 1674/5, Billerica, MA	——	20 Sept. 1689, Billerica, MA
6. Hannah	18 Dec. 1681, Billerica, MA	——	

Pioneers of Billerica • *Settling the Shawshine Wilderness: 1654-1660*

Ralph Hill, Jr., Captain

b.	*before 1633, England*
emig.	-----
m.	*15 November 1660, Martha Toothaker, Billerica, MA*
d.	*9 April 1695, Billerica, MA*

With his father, the senior Ralph Hill, Ralph Jr. settled in Billerica @1654. He was one of the signers of the Shawshine Agreement to separate from Cambridge, MA and call the town Billerica. At first, Ralph had property on Andover Road, but sold this to another founding father John Poulter in 1658. In 1656, Ralph bought the farm south of his father's, close to Nutting Pond and east of the Concord Road. He built a garrison house which was used during King Philip's War in 1675/6. The townspeople advised to use the fortification were: the Hills, Thomas Dutton, Jr., William French, William and Isaac Chamberlaine and two soldiers.

In 1660, Hill and James Kidder were appointed by the town of Billerica to join with Chelmsford workmen to repair the large bridge over the Concord River on the route to Chelmsford. The bridge soon needed to be repaired again, for four years later another team from Chelmsford and Billerica remedied new concerns over its safety.

Among his other activities in 1661, Hill and an Indian male called John each received one pound for the killing of wolves within the bounds of the town. Since each wolf was valued at 20 shillings, the two men killed 10 wolves that time.

Ralph Hill married his stepmother's daughter Martha Toothaker; the daughter of Roger Toothaker, Sr. The couple married 15 November 1660 in Billerica. They had six children over a 20-year period: four daughters, Elizabeth, Deborah, Rebecca and Hannah, and two sons, Samuel and Daniel.

Ralph served in the town militia as a sergeant, and later rose to the position of Captain for which he was titled from then on. He was a deputy of the town to stand guard against the Indian uprisings in 1692/3.

The home of Ralph Hill.

The Salem Witch Trials involved Martha's brother Dr. Roger Toothaker and Roger's wife's family. One can imagine that this episode in the family's lives was most disturbing and stressful for the humiliation and the prejudices of the community. Ralph died only a couple years after this family crisis: 9 April 1695 in Billerica. He wrote a very detailed will 2 April 1695 [Middlesex Pro. #11503], and had completed his own inventory of his estate a year before 30 March 1694. His sons Samuel and Daniel were to be executors and were clearly told to take care of their mother's welfare. While she was his widow, she was to have a room in the homestead, a horse, two milk cows, cellar space for 10 bushels of Indian corn, three bushels of rye, two bushels of malt, one bushel of wheat, a barrel of cider, 12 bushels of apples, six pounds of sheep wool, 12 pounds of flax and two swine. This list of items was to be renewed yearly.

Ralph gave the homestead to his eldest son Samuel, who was also to pay the legacies to his sisters. Daniel was given the property at the Shawshin River.

Hill had previously given monies to his daughters: Elizabeth, Deborah and Mary of £34 each as well as "household stuff". He willed that £20 be given to Elizabeth Baldin in four payments, grandsons: Ralph and Timothy Baldin were each to have 40 shillings, and Samuel Sheldon was to have a similar amount when he came of age. Cousin Samuel Kitredge was to acquire a house and lot in Billerica.

Cousin John French, Cornet John Stern and Joseph Tompson were overseers of the will.

Founding Father
RALPH HILL, SR.

m. (1) ———
b. ———
d. Before 1638, England

Children	Born	Married	Died
1. Jane	———, England	———, Francis Littlefield	20 Dec. 1846, ———
2. Ralph	Before 1633, England	15 Nov. 1660, Martha Toothaker	1695, ———

Pioneers of Billerica • Settling the Shawshine Wilderness: 1654-1660

Ralph Hill, Senior

b.	-----, *Billercay, England*
emig.	*before 1638*
m.	*(1) --------, England*
	(2) 21 December 1638, Margaret Toothaker, Plymouth, MA
d.	*29 April 1663, --------*
bu.	*Old South Bury Ground, Billerica, MA*

Ralph Hill, Sr. and his son Ralph Hill, Jr. were two of the earliest colonizers to move to Shawshine, MA, arriving by 1655. They both requested the court of the county to separate Shawshine from Cambridge and grant that they be able to call it Billerica, after their former hometown in England.

Ralph, Sr. sailed into the Plymouth Colony with a wife and two children: Jane and Ralph, Jr. In 1638, he was called a yeoman, or one of the upper middle class who owned property. Ralph sold his house and garden in Plymouth 16 September 1643 to Stephen Wood for £12 to move to Woburn, where he was made a Freeman 26 May 1647. Two of his primary reasons for relocation were more property availability and a more relaxed religious agenda. In 1649, Hill was chosen a Woburn selectman.

We have not learned the name of Ralph's first wife, but the couple had their children in England or soon after landing in America. Before 1638, Ralph's first wife died and Ralph married at Plymouth, the widow Margaret (--------) Toothaker, who had two children: Roger and Martha. Margaret's previous husband was Roger Toothaker, Sr., who died soon after the family's September 1635 arrival in America on the ship "Hopewell." When her first husband died, Margaret acquired a property called Wellingland at Woburn Plains, MA.

Ralph, Sr. and Margaret had three children together: Nathaniel, Jonathan and Rebecca. In 1660, Margaret's daughter Martha married Ralph Hill, Jr.

Ralph Hill, Sr. relocated to Shawshine in 1655 and chose a tract on Dudley's Farm, south of Charnstaffe Lane, west of the Concord Road and a mile south west of the village.

Pioneers of Billerica • Settling the Shawshine Wilderness: 1654-1660

Founding Father

RALPH HILL, SR.

m. (2) -----, Margaret Toothaker, widow of Roger Toothaker, Sr.
b. 1595, England
emig. September 1635
d. 22 Nov. 1683, Billerica, MA

Children	Born	Married	Died
3. Nathaniel	c.1642, Plymouth, MA	1667, Elizabeth Holmes	14 May 1706, Chelmsford, MA
4. Jonathan	20 Apr. 1646, Woburn, MA	1666, Mary Hartwell	After 1710, Billerica, MA
5. Rebecca	-----	1666, Caleb Farley	1669, Billerica, MA

A respected elder of the community, Hill was made a church deacon in 1661. Ralph wrote his will 18 November 1662, which was proven 12 September 1663 [Middlesex Probate: #11502].

Ralph, Sr. willed his wife Margaret one third of the estate and meadows in Billerica, a bed, a cow, two pigs and a horse to ride. If she chose to remarry, she was to have only £3 a year paid by their sons Nathaniel and Jonathan, the executors.

Hill listed his children and gifts to them: Ralph, Jr. was to have £23, Martha £20, Rebecca £30, Nathaniel the land towards Concord and one half of the Billerica property, Jonathan the other properties, his grandchildren: Mary Littlefield £15, and Elizabeth Hill 20 shillings at age 12. Ralph, Sr. also noted his son-in-law Roger Toothaker, who was bequeathed 33 acres of land in the common field.

Ralph Hill, Sr. was the first person to be buried in the Old South Bury Ground in Billerica, one half acre of land he gave the town April 1663.

Pioneers of Billerica • Settling the Shawshine Wilderness: 1654-1660

The Old South Burying Ground on Concord Road in Billerica, the gift of Ralph Hill.

Pioneers of Billerica • Settling the Shawshine Wilderness: 1654-1660

Founding Father

THOMAS HUBBARD

Son of James Hubbard, a brother James

m. ----, Elizabeth Huitt

b. ----

d. ----

Children	Born	Married	Died
None			

Pioneers of Billerica • Settling the Shawshine Wilderness: 1654-1660

Thomas Hubbard

b.   10 August 1638, Watertown, MA
m.   15 October 1662, Elizabeth Huitt, Billerica, MA
d.   9 November 1662, Billerica, MA

Thomas was the son of Sarah and James Hubbard of Cambridge, who had two sons and a daughter Sarah who married Samuel Champney, a founding father. When his mother was widowed, she married William Hamlet, another founding father of Billerica.

In 1660, Thomas acquired a 32-acre home lot and about 75 upland acres in Billerica on the north side of the township. It was on the west side of Roger's land, by the Concord Road, and to its west, the property fell into a pond.

Thomas married Elizabeth Huitt on 15 October 1662 in Billerica. Her ancestry is unknown, but a Thomas Huitt of Hull, MA, who had emigrated from Lincoln, England close to the date of 7 October 1647, empowered an attorney to collect rents.

Death came early to Hubbard; for he was only 24 years of age and just married when he died 9 November 1662.

On 9 December 1662, an inventory was conducted on Hubbard's estate. He had a house and lot valued at £60, two cows and very little other material possessions, valued at £49.

There were many creditors (£30) and the court first stipulated that his widow Elizabeth would receive a dowry, his brother James one third of the estate, and his sister one third. On 20 October 1663, it was determined that Elizabeth would have the full estate [Middlesex Probate #12201].

Founding Father

HENRY JEFTS

m. (1) 13 Sept. 1647, Anna Stowers, Woburn, MA
b. ——
d. ——

Children	Born	Married	Died

Pioneers of Billerica • Settling the Shawshine Wilderness: 1654-1660

Henry Jefts

b.   *@1606, England*
m.   *(1) 13 September 1647, Anna Stowers, Woburn, MA*
         (2) 21 May 1649, Hannah Births, Woburn, MA
         (3) 3 October 1666, Mary (--------) Bird, Billerica, MA
         (4) 5 May 1681, Mary Baker, Billerica, MA
d.   *24 May 1700, --------*

Henry Jefts was an early settler of Billerica, MA, arriving in the region between 1652-4. He chose one of the 12 sections of the Dudley Farm, which was equivalent to 125 acres. Thirteen of this was meadow and 112 acres was upland. His home was near Indian Hill north west of Nuttings Pond.

He was a representative of Shawshine to the Cambridge Court in 1654 to separate this area from the mother township in England and call it Billerica.

Henry Jefts came to Shawshine with his second wife, the former Hannah Births. She was probably a sister to Christian Births, who was married to George Farley, another founding father. Since Christian was born in Sweden, and sailed to America with her father who died enroute, this birthplace is suggested for Hannah.

Henry had previously been married to Anna Stowers in Woburn in 1647. Although not a daughter, she may have been related to Nicholas Stowers of Dorchester, MA. Anna probably died in 1648, for Henry married Hannah Births in Woburn 21 May 1649.

Pioneers of Billerica • Settling the Shawshine Wilderness: 1654-1660

Founding Father

HENRY JEFTS

m. (2) 21 May 1649, Hannah Births, Woburn, MA
b. ——, probably Sweden
d. 15 Sept. 1662, Billerica, MA

Children	Born	Married	Died
1. John	11 May 1651, Woburn, MA	1688, Lydia Fish	28 Sept. 1712, Billerica, MA
2. Hannah	——, Billerica, MA	——	May 1653, Billerica, MA
3. Hannah	4 Feb. 1654/5, Billerica, MA	1679, Andrew Spalding, A deacon	21 Jan. 1729/30, Chelmsford, MA
4. Joanna	24 May 1656, Billerica, MA	(1) 1690, John Dunkin, Died of smallpox, Billerica, MA (2) ——, Benjamin Dutton	1 Aug. 1692, Billerica, MA, Killed with two children by Indians
5. Henry	21 Mar. 1658/9, Billerica, MA	——, Mary Baldwin	9 Nov. 1704, Billerica, MA

Pioneers of Billerica • Settling the Shawshine Wilderness: 1654-1660

Henry and Hannah had five children, one of whom died in infancy. Hannah died in Billerica 15 September 1662.

Four years later, Henry married Mary (--------) Bird, the widow of Simon Bird, a founding father. When Simon died, Henry was administrator for his friend. Simon left a list of creditors unpaid. Following the marriage of Henry and Mary, the couple left the Dudley Farm property to move to Long Street (Boston Road) in the village. Mary died 1 April 1679, without having any children in either of her marriages. Following Mary's death in 1679, Jefts deeded portions of the Bird land to fill the expectations of Simon's will and to pay debts, especially to the church and Rev. Whiting [Mdsx. Court File 87].

For his fourth marriage, Henry married Mary Baker of Concord 5 May 1681.

He composed his will 2 March 1692, proven 17 June 1700, following his death 14 May 1700. He bequeathed his eldest son John the property he lived on, inclusive of buildings, orchard and 10 acres of additional land and swamp. Son Henry also received a property with buildings he purchased of William Champney and 10 acres of land "so far as Concord Road." Also listed were his daughters: Hannah Spalding, Johanna Dutton; grandchildren, Mary and John Dunkin; Henry, son of Andrew Spalding; Alice, John, Mary and Hannah Jefts; and son-in-law William Baker of Concord, MA [Mdsx. Prob. #B12519].

Pioneers of Billerica • Settling the Shawshine Wilderness: 1654-1660

Founding Father

HENRY JEFTS

m. (3)   3 Oct. 1666, Mary Bird, Billerica, MA

b. ----

d. 1 Apr. 1679, Billerica, MA

Children	Born	Married	Died

Pioneers of Billerica • Settling the Shawshine Wilderness: 1654-1660

Founding Father
HENRY JEFTS

m. (4) 5 May 1681, Mary Baker, Billerica, MA
b. ——, Concord, MA
d. ——

Children	Born	Married	Died

Pioneers of Billerica • Settling the Shawshine Wilderness: 1654-1660

Founding Father
SAMUEL KEMP

m. ———, Sarah Foster, daughter of Thomas and Elizabeth Foster, a founding family
b. ———
d. ———

Children	Born	Married	Died
1. Samuel	23 Feb. 1662/3, Billerica, MA	———	dy
2. Abigail, *twins*	27 Mar. 1665, Billerica, MA	1686, James Broad	———, Groton, MA
3. Samuel, *twins*	27 Mar. 1665, Billerica, MA	———, Susannah Lawrence	after 1707, Groton, MA
4. Jonathan	6 Apr. 1668, Groton, MA	(1) 1698, Mary Gilson	3 Apr. 1752, Chelmsford, MA
		(2) 1718, Sarah Gilson	
5. Mehitabel	4 Jan. 1673, Groton, MA	1693, Moses Keyse	16 Apr. 1768, Chelmsford, MA
6. Bethiah	9 July 1683, Groton, MA	———	———

Pioneers of Billerica • Settling the Shawshine Wilderness: 1654-1660

Samuel Kemp

b.   *?1638, --------*
m.   *23 May 1662, Sarah Foster, Billerica, MA*
d.   *after 1683, Groton, MA*

A nine-year resident of Billerica, Samuel Kemp was granted a five-acre lot, i.e. half a single share of land or 70 acres, on Loes Plain in 1658. His log cabin was near the intersection of Allen Street and Baldwin. Samuel chose to sell his property in 1669 to Thomas Ross to move to Groton, MA, where he was employed as a surveyor.

Kemp achieved recognition for signing a petition in March 1658 with Samuel Foster and Edward Kemp to trade with the local Indian tribe. He was also known for having musical talents, and on 24 October 1661 was elected drummer for the town's militia called the "Trayne Band."

Samuel married Sarah Foster of Braintree and Billerica, MA in 1662, and had six children with her. Sarah was the daughter of Thomas Foster, one of the founding fathers.

Samuel Kemp did not leave a will.

Founding Father

JAMES KIDDER

Son of James Kidder of Sussex, England

m. ------, Anna Moore, daughter of Elder Francis and Katharine Moore who migrated to Cambridge, MA

    b. c.1630, England

    d. ------

Children	Born	Married	Died
1. Hannah	1 Mar. 1650/1, Cambridge, MA	1672, Nathaniel Kettle A surveyor	1699, Charlestown, MA
2. Dorothy	29 Jan. 1652, Cambridge, MA	1673, Jonathan Hyde	Before 1724, Canterbury, CT
3. James	3 Jan. 1653/4, Cambridge, MA	1678, Elizabeth Brown	15 Dec. 1732, Billerica, MA
4. John	1655/6, Cambridge, MA	1684, Lydia Parker	27 Oct. 1731, Chelmsford, MA
5. Thomas	1 Mar. 1657, Cambridge, MA A Captain	------, Elizabeth ------	------, Watertown, MA
6. Nathaniel	27 Feb. 1658/9, Cambridge, MA	------	7 Jan. 1690/1, Newtown, MA
7. Ephraim	31 Aug. 1660, Billerica, MA	(1) 1685, Rachel Crosby (2) 1724, Elizabeth Cary	25 Sept. 1724, Billerica, MA
8. Stephen	26 Nov. 1662, Billerica, MA A blacksmith	c.1693, Mary Johnson Died of smallpox	5 July 1748, Charlestown, MA
9. Enoch	16 Sept. 1664, Billerica, MA	(1) 1685, Mary Heywood (2) 1743, Hannah Danforth	1 Dec. 1752, Billerica, MA
10. Samuel	7 Jan. 1665/6, Billerica, MA Had a malt mill	1689, Sarah Griggs	4 July 1724, Cambridge, MA
11. Sarah	1 June 1667, Billerica, MA	1689/90, George Brown A Captain	27 Feb. 1717/8, Billerica, MA
12. Joseph	20 Nov. 1670, Billerica, MA	------	1683, Billerica, MA

Pioneers of Billerica • Settling the Shawshine Wilderness: 1654-1660

James Kidder

b.	*1626 East Grimstead, Sussex, England*
emig.	*@1649*
m.	*1649/50, Anna Moore, Cambridge, MA*
d.	*16 April 1676, Billerica, MA*

James Kidder tragically died following King Philip's War 16 April 1676, where it was believed he had been wounded. He had held the position of Ensign in Captain Danforth's militia. He was just 50 years old and left a wife and 12 children, six of them minors. His death also left a gap in Billerica's activities for he had been predominant in church affairs, in opening his home as a garrison during the War, was a juror in the Cambridge Court in 1662, and was a selectman and surveyor in Billerica.

James was born at East Grimstead, Sussex, England in 1626. He emigrated to America about 1649, and soon after married the Englishwoman Anna Moore, daughter of Elder Francis and Katharine Moore.

Kidder and his family first settled in Cambridge, MA where James was active in the Church of England. Between 1650 and 1656, he had property on the north shore of French Pond and Menotomy River, Arlington, MA.

In 1656, Kidder bought considerable property in Billerica, MA, but did not move to town until 1658. He had a 30-acre tract by the Common, 26 acres on Loes Plain, 60 acres on Fox Hill, 39 acres on Heath Brook in Tewskbury, MA, various meadows and more. Billerica enlisted James Kidder and Ralph Hill, Jr. to repair the bridge over the Concord River to Chelmsford in 1660.

James built a large home on River Street at Boston Road for his 12 children. This home was fortified as a garrison for the Indian problems in 1675. In 1676, James Kidder died without a will. An inventory was made in 1677 of his property, which was valued at £370. The land had much value as well as his horses, cows, pigs, poultry, clothing, chests and a cupboard [Inventory #13232].

Eight years later, his widow Anna remarried to William Underwood of Chelmsford, MA.

Founding Father

SAMUEL KINSLEY
Son of Stephen Kinsley

m.   c.1656, Hanah Bracket, daughter of Richard Bracket
     bp. 4 June 1634, Boston, MA
     Her second husband was John Blanchard
     d. 2 July 1706, Dunstable, MA; killed by Indians

Children	Born	Married	Died
1. Hannah	27 May 1656, Braintree, MA	-----	-----
2. Elizabeth	22 Sept. 1657, Braintree, MA	1680, John Cummings	1706, -------
3. Mary	-----	-----	26 Mar. 1659, --------
4. Samuel	23 Nov. 1660, Braintree, MA	-----	19 Nov. 1661, Braintree, MA

Pioneers of Billerica • *Settling the Shawshine Wilderness: 1654-1660*

Samuel Kinsley

b.   *-----, Braintree, MA*
m.   *@1656, Hanah Bracket, --------*
d.   *21 May 1662 Billerica, MA*

In August 1659, Samuel Kinsley was granted a 125-acre upland tract and a very large 100-acre house lot, along Andover Road, south of the 320-foot Fox Hill. He married Hanah Bracket, the sister of Peter and John Bracket, founding fathers, @1656. They had four children: Elizabeth, Hannah, Mary and Samuel. Samuel died as a young man on 21 May 1662 in Billerica.

An inventory was made of Samuel's estate (no date) and probated 15 June 1662 for Hanah and the children [Middlesex Probate 2:93-4 + ALS #2552]. The house and land were valued at £70, out of a total evaluation of £103.03.0.

Kinsley's wife Hanah remarried to John Blanchard of Dunstable, MA. Blanchard died in 1693 and Hanah was killed 2 July 1706 during an Indian uprising in Dunstable.

Founding Father
JOHN KITTREDGE

m. ———, Mary Littlefield of Woburn, MA, ———
Daughter of Jane (Hill) and Francis Littlefield
b. 14 Dec. 1646, ———
d. 17 Oct. 1719, ———

Children	Born	Married	Died
1. John	24 Jan. 1665/6, Billerica, MA A doctor	1665, Hannah French	27 Apr. 1714, Billerica, MA
2. James	21 Mar. 1667/8, Billerica, MA	(1) ———, Sarah Fowle (2) 1708, Mary Abbott	———
3. Daniel	22 July 1670, Billerica, MA A deacon	1694, Elizabeth Foster	4 Mar. 1741/2, Billerica, MA
4. Jonathan	16 July 1674, Billerica, MA	———	23 Mar. 1696, Billerica, MA
5. Benoni	2 May 1677, Billerica, MA	———	———

Pioneers of Billerica • Settling the Shawshine Wilderness: 1654-1660

★

John Kitterige (Kittridge)

b.   *1630, England*
emig. *@1660*
m.   *2 November 1664, Mary Littlefield, Billerica, MA*
d.   *18 October 1676, Billerica, MA*

In September 1660, John Kitterige was employed with founding father John Parker as his master in Billerica, MA. Presumably his position was that of an indentured servant,

where he could or had worked off the transport agreement from England. His first grant of land was five acres, and he then acquired a small house lot of 10 acres on the south side of Bare Hill, on the west side of Boston Road, adjoining Robert Parker's lot south of the village. He also was given four acres of meadow. In July 1663, he acquired more land next to that which he already owned, whereby he could have a shop.

In his history of Billerica, Hazen does not define what kind of shop John had. However, Kitterige had skills as a medical practitioner and surgeon. Because he did not have a medical education as required for practice in England, when the authorities learned of his activities, he was forced to flee his homeland. It has been said he was a man of great courage and Herculean strength, but also learned in anatomy. He may have acquired this knowledge from his own study of the skeleton and broken bones.

One of his descendants, Mabel Kittredge, alleged that on the crossing to America, John—perhaps out of necessity— was in charge of the ship transport and passengers.

Pioneers of Billerica • Settling the Shawshine Wilderness: 1654-1660

A Few Diseases and Treatment in the Sixteenth Century

AGUE — Intermittent fever from March to July with chills and/or sweating. Thought to be caused by the warmth of the sun acting on humors that accumulated in the blood in the winter.

CATARRAH — A cold with cough, fever, watery eyes, runny nose, thirst. Treat with the syrup of the fern Maidenhair, or wormwood, sage, marigolds and crab-claws boiled in a sweet, spicy milk drink curdled with ale or wine called a posset.

CHOLERA INFANTUM — Vomiting, diarrhea, fever, prostration in young children during summer and autumn. Death usually occurred in 3-5 days.

COLIC — A "dry bellyache". Treat with herbs put into a bag that is laid on the belly, followed by a cordial julip with "poppy" juice in it.

FLUX — Abdominal pain with diarrhea, blood, mucus. If the physician determined it was amoebic flux, the new treatment was to cause vomiting with Ipecacuanhe. Another treatment for the belly gripping was pills made from sugar, salad oil and cotton boiled thick.

GOUT — Joints painful from deposits of urates. Make a poultice of the herb mallows cut small and boiled in wine vinegar. Add rye bran, a hot moist plaster of frog spawn, and a purge of senna powder.

PLEURISY — Inflammation of the membrane in the chest with chills, fever, dry cough and pain. Pulverize coriander and carduus seed with harthair, put one dram in a cup of wine.

QUINSY — Inposthumation of almonds for an acute inflammation of the tonsils.

SCROFULA — Also called King's Evil. Tuberculosis in the skin from the underlying lymph nodes seen mostly in children and young adults. At the time, it was believed that the disease could be cured by the touch of England's King.

In Billerica, Kitterige not only expressed his concerns for the villagers who had medical problems, but also for the loose animals. He was given the responsibility for framing the swine with a yoke and placing a ring in their noses so they could be tethered.

John acquired property in Tewksbury in 1661, where his descendants then made their home. This property was 64 acres on the east side of Alewife Brook, south of the highway to Globe Hill, which was beyond Pattenville, near the Shawshin River.

Kitterige married Mary Littlefield of Woburn, MA, the daughter of Jane (Hill) and Francis Littlefield. Her parents removed to Wells, Maine about the time of the Kitterige marriage. John and Mary had five children, all sons. His oldest son was Dr. John Kitterige, who married Hannah French.

John died 18 October 1676 in Billerica. An inventory of his estate was completed [Middlesex Probate #B13372; Vol. 5, p. 33]. Enumerated were household utensils and furnishings, a pair of pistols and cutlass, two steers, four cows, a black horse and 18 acres of land with the homestead and barn, plus meadows west of Concord River and at Prospect. In addition, he had 25 acres of upland at Content Playne, 36 acres in the Old Common Field and 12 acres south of Shawshin River.

Mary married for the second time in 1677/8 to founding father John French, after she required financial aid from the town. She was John's fourth wife. John French was the father-in-law of her son John Kitterige. Her son's wife Hannah then became a daughter-in-law twice over through the two marriages. In his will, Ralph Hill, Sr. called Mary Kitterige French his granddaughter.

Founding Father

JOHN MARSHALL (MARSHAL)

(1) ———, Hannah Atkinson, ———
    b. 5 Mar. 1644, Concord, MA
    Daughter of Thomas Atkinson
    d. 7 Sept. 1665, Billerica, MA

Children	Born	Married	Died

Pioneers of Billerica • Settling the Shawshine Wilderness: 1654-1660

John Marshall ★

John Marshal

b.   ?1632, --------
m.   (1) 19 November 1662, Hannah Atkinson, Billerica, MA
            (2) 27 November 1665, Mary Burrage, --------
            (3) 30 November 1681, Damaris Waite, Billerica, MA
d.   5 November 1702, Billerica, MA

John Marshal was granted about 75 acres in Billerica 4 February 1656-7. He later sold this parcel to Dr. James Frost. It was near the "old" Andover Road, near the Commons and John Sheldon's land in the center of Loes Plain. John later acquired property further east on Loes Plain at Baldwin Road. Hs road was called Marshall's Lane and the homestead was still standing there in 1882.

John Marshal married three times. His first wife was Hannah Atkinson, thought to be the daughter of Thomas Atkinson of Concord, MA. She died three years after their marriage. They had no children.

His second wife was Mary Burrage, with whom John had nine boys and girls. Only two of his children survived infancy: Johanna and John, Jr. Mary died in 1680 a few weeks after childbirth.

The following year he married Damaris Waite, widow of Alexander Waite of Malden, MA.

John Marshal died 5 November 1702 in Billerica. His intestate will [Mdsx. Pro. #14708] was probated 28 December 1702 by John Marshal, Jr. Two other names mentioned in the presentation were Peter Corneal of Billerica, a son-in-law, and Thomas Stacy, blacksmith of Cambridge. He was to be the third husband of Damaris Marshal.

The items in the inventory were primarily household furnishings, clothing, small arms, a house and buildings valued at £100 and various meadows and upland valued at £52.

Founding Father

JOHN MARSHALL (MARSHAL)

(2) ——, Mary Burrage, ——

b. 3 Oct. 1641, ——

Daughter of John Burrage. Sister of Hannah, who married John French.

d. 30 Oct. 1680, Billerica, MA

Children	Born	Married	Died
1. John	7 June 1667, Billerica, MA	——	7 July 1667, Billerica, MA
2. Mary	2 Oct. 1668, Billerica, MA	——	17 July 1669, Billerica, MA
3. Johana	1 Apr. 1670, Billerica, MA	1695, Peter Corneal	28 Dec. 1704, Billerica, MA
4. John, Jr.	1 Aug. 1671, Billerica, MA	1695/6, Unis Rogers	25 Jan. 1713/4, Billerica, MA
5. Mary	14 Oct. 1672, Billerica, MA	——	18 Oct. 1673, Billerica, MA
6. Hannah	18 Feb. 1673/4, Billerica, MA	——	21 Oct. 1674, Billerica, MA
7. Thomas	bp. 10 Nov. 1675, Charlestown, MA	——	20 Nov. 1675, Billerica, MA
8. Isabel	31 Jan. 1677/8, Billerica, MA	——	28 Apr. 1677/8, Billerica, MA
9. Mehittabel	13 Aug. 1680, Billerica, MA		Aug. 1680, Billerica, MA

Pioneers of Billerica • Settling the Shawshine Wilderness: 1654-1660

123

Founding Father

JOHN MARSHALL (MARSHALL)

(3) ———, Damaris Waite, ———
b. 5 Mar. 1644, Concord, MA
Widow of Alexander Waite from Malden, MA. Her third marriage was to Thomas Johnson 1703.
d. ———, Andover, MA

Children	Born	Married	Died

Pioneers of Billerica • Settling the Shawshine Wilderness: 1654-1660

Pioneers of Billerica • Settling the Shawshine Wilderness: 1654-1660

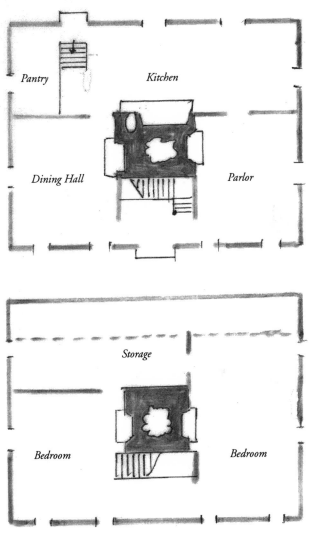

Typical layout of a 17th century home.

Pioneers of Billerica • Settling the Shawshine Wilderness: 1654-1660

Founding Father
GOULDIN MOORE

m.　(1)　Joanne (———) Champney, widow of John Champney
　　　　Brother to Elder Richard Champney
　　　b. c.1610-5, ———
　　　d. 18 Feb. 1675/6, Billerica, MA

Children	Born	Married	Died
1. Hanah	15 Sept. 1643, Cambridge, MA	1665/6, John Hastings	10 Jun. 1667, Cambridge, MA
2. Lydia	1645, Cambridge, MA	1669, Caleb Farley	1715, Billerica, MA
3. Ruth	164-, Cambridge, MA	1670, Daniel Shed	1730, Billerica, MA
Joanne's children with John Champney			
1. Mary	Oct. 1635, Cambridge, MA	———, Theophilus Richardson	——
2. Sarah	May 1636, ———	———, John Russell, Jr.	——
3. John	28 May 1641, ———		20 Feb. 1664/5, ———

Pioneers of Billerica • Settling the Shawshine Wilderness: 1654-1660

Gouldin Moore

b.   *@1609, England*
emig.   -----
m.   *@1643, Joanne (--------) Champney, Cambridge, MA*
d.   *3 September 1698, Billerica, MA*

Perhaps in 1643, at the age of 34 or so, Gouldin Moore married Joanne (--------)
Champney, a widow with three minor children: Mary b. 1635, Sarah b. 1638,
John b. 1641. Her previous marriage had been with John Champney @1635, a brother
to Elder Richard Champney, a founding father. John and Joanne had acquired property
in Cambridge, MA and she had joined the church there. In 1646, her brother-in-law
Elder Richard was granted permission in Cambridge to repair his "Brother" Gouldin
Moore's house and barn. Richard Champney also assisted Joanne to sell the properties
of her late husband [MBCR.3:217].

In 1658, Gouldin, Joanne, her Champney
children and the three Moore youngsters moved
to Billerica, where they bought James Parker's
original grant, with a house lot of 14 acres.
They later acquired nine more acres. The land
was on both sides of Andover Road, central to
the village in 1661, with the road itself bisecting
the property.

Joanne and Gouldin had three children:
Hanah, Lydia and Ruth. Joanne died 18
February 1675/6 , perhaps about 60 years old.
Gouldin died in Billerica 3 September 1698,
approximately 89 years of age.
He did not leave a will.

Founding Father

JAMES PARKER

m. (1) ——, Elizabeth Long, daughter of Sarah (Taylor) and Robert Long
b. ——, St. Albans, Hertfordshire, England
d. ——

Children	Born	Married	Died
1. Elizabeth	12 Mar. 1645, Woburn, MA	——, William Gary	——, Roxbury, MA
2. Ann	5 Mar. 1647, Woburn, MA	1670, Nathaniel Blood	1728, Chelmsford/Groton, MA
3. John	18 Feb. 1649, Woburn, MA	Married, ——	Before 7 Apr.1679, Groton, MA
4. Sarah	29 Aug. 1650, Woburn, MA	——	15 Sept. 1704, Groton, MA
5. Joseph	1651, Woburn, MA	(1) ——, Elizabeth Blood?	After 1701, Groton, MA
		(2) 1696, Hannah Bake	
6. James	15 Apr. 1652, Woburn, MA	——, Mary Parker	27 July 1694, ——
			Killed with his family by Indians
7. Josiah	1655, Chelmsford, MA	1678, Elizabeth Saxton	1731, ——
8. Samuel	1656, Chelmsford, MA	——, Abigail Lake	1712, Groton, MA
9. Josheware	13 Mar. 1658, Chelmsford, MA	1690, Abigail (Shattuck) Morse	1691, Groton, MA
10. Zechariah	14 Jan. 1659, Chelmsford, MA	——, Elizabeth Page	Before 1700, Groton, MA
11. Eleazor	9 Nov. 1661, Chelmsford, MA	——, Mehitable Barron	——, Groton, MA

Pioneers of Billerica • Settling the Shawshine Wilderness: 1654-1660

James Parker, Captain

b.	*@1617, Great Burstead, England*
emig.	-----
m.	*(1) 23 May 1643, Elizabeth Long, Woburn, MA*
	(2) -----, Eunice (Brooks) Carter, --------
d.	*shortly before 12 July 1700, Groton, MA*

In the beginning days of the settlement at Shawshine, there were many Parkers: John, Abram, Joseph, Jacob and James, who at that time or later became associated with the village and outlying areas. Along with John and Robert, James Parker requested that Shawshine separate from Cambridge, MA in 1654 and be called Billerica.

James was one of the initial grantees of the Dudley Farm: a vast acreage that encompassed Indian Hill, Nutting Pond and the woods all the way to the Concord River. He had moved up to the farm from Woburn, MA with his wife Elizabeth and six young children.

The family stayed in Billerica only a couple years, for in 1658 James sold his parcel to Gouldin Moore. While in Billerica he was an agent for heirs of the Winthrop Farm with its large meadow (in present day Bedford, MA).

James and his brother Joseph moved to Chelmsford, MA where Elizabeth gave birth to five more sons. In the summer of 1661, James' wife was pregnant with their last child and was managing to raise 11 other sons and daughters under the age of 16. During this time, Joseph and James were scouting for new lands to the west of Chelmsford by 10 to 12 miles, and located the virgin woodlands of Groton, MA. This area is hillier terrain, with many enormous pines as well as the more common hardwoods. Southeast of Groton is a granite area, and Groton itself has many steep, forested ridge slopes left by glaciers.

Between 1664 and 1666, James Parker acquired an immense amount of land. His home was in the center of Groton, next to the Town Hall on the west side of Main Street. His property extended all the way to the east to include Baddacock Pond (two miles from the village), Gibbet Hill and Brown Loaf Hill.

Founding Father

JAMES PARKER

m. (2) ----, Eunice (Brooks) Carter, daughter of John and Eunice (Mousall) Brooks
    b. 10 Oct. 1655, Woburn, MA
    First married to Rev. Samuel Carter
    d. ?Nov. 1721, Groton, MA

Children	Born	Married	Died
12. Sarah	12 Dec. 1697, Groton, MA	----	After 1700, ------

PARKER HOUSE

NEAR BY STOOD A GARRISON
HOUSE. RESIDENCE OF CAPTAIN
JAMES PARKER. COMMANDER OF
THE TOWN FORCES IN KING PHILIP'S
WAR. HERE CAPTAIN PARKER PAR-
LEYED WITH THE INDIAN CHIEF JOHN
MONOCO REGARDING HIS THREAT TO
BURN GROTON AND BOSTON. MARCH
13, 1676.
MASSACHUSETTS BAY COLONY
TERCENTENARY COMMISSION

James was the most "prominent" man in town, to quote Samuel Green, historian. Although a scholarly person, Parker was more noticed for being on every committee and in every meeting. He lay out boundaries and roads, helped plan and set up a corn mill in 1667 and saw to the contract for the bridge to Billerica and Chelmsford which was built by Job Lane of Billerica in 1667.

The Parkers built a large home to accommodate their children, but also to use as a garrison.

Parker had military experience and was Captain of the militia. In 1675, there were about 60 families in Groton and five garrisons, most of which were in the center of town. With Indian tensions increasing at an alarming rate, James was very disturbed by the scarcity of ammunition, guns and food in the village. In March 1676, there was an Indian raid where 400 natives took out their hostility on a number of Massachusetts communities. That month, Captain Parker sat down with his "old neighbor" Indian Chief Monaco to try to find resolution and a peaceful solution to their differences. Chief Monoco shared his reasons for warring on the settlers, and how there could be peace if things were done his way. Monaco boasted he had burned down the towns of Medfield and Lancaster, MA. He was ready to gain more satisfaction from the white man "What me will, Me do" [Shultz and Tougias, King Philip's War, p. 202].

The town was spared, but Groton had a very different ending during the Indian Wars of 1691/2. The garrisons all filled up with the villagers, while the Indians attacked and fired repeated volleys at the fortifications. There were 11 men in the Parker garrison shooting back, which convinced the Indians to retreat from the house. However, the Nipmuck tribesmen vented their rage and burned down 40 other houses in town. The community had to be abandoned, with many of the inhabitants residing and recovering from their tragedy in Concord, MA.

James was town clerk in Groton 1678-9, town treasurer in 1697, a representative to the General Court of Middlesex County for Groton in 1683, deacon of the Groton church in 1693, and its first selectman 1662-1699.

Pioneers of Billerica • Settling the Shawshine Wilderness: 1654-1660

James Parker wrote his will in Groton 25 May 1700 and died shortly before 12 July when it was proven. He noted his wife Eunice, daughters Sarah Parker, Anna Blood and Elizabeth Gary. He also listed his grandchildren: Elizabeth Parker, the daughter of his son Zechariah, and Abiel Parker, daughter of Joshua, who was deceased. James stated that before the writing of the will he made gifts to his sons: James, Josiah, Zechariah, Eleazor and Samuel. Josiah Parker was the executor.

Pioneers of Billerica • Settling the Shawshine Wilderness: 1654-1660

Founding Father

JOHN PARKER

m.   23 June 1642, Mary (Pope) Poulter Aylett in Essex, England.

b. ——

d. ——

Children	Born	Married	Died
None			

Pioneers of Billerica • Settling the Shawshine Wilderness: 1654-1660

John Parker

b.	*4 June 1615, Great Burstead, Essex, England*
emig.	*after June 1642*
m.	*-----, Mary (?Pope) Poulter Aylett, Essex, England*
d.	*14 June 1667, Billerica, MA*

A very early settler of Billerica, John Parker leased and worked the Cambridge Church farm of 700 acres on both sides of the Shawshin River, north of the Woburn Road for a rent of £100. In 1653, John settled into a home south of Webb's Brook in Billerica, MA. He arrived from Woburn with his wife Mary and her two children from a previous marriage, and his brothers: James and Joseph. John and Mary did not have children of their own.

John was a reliable, steadfast man who was vitally interested in Billerica. In 1654, he was one of the signers of the request at Cambridge for separation and to use Billerica as the name of the town. Parker was the first town clerk and the first tax collector. He arranged for two large grants of land to be sold; with the money used for the town's advantage and to pay off Cambridge claims.

When the community decided it needed a meetinghouse for church services c. 1660, John built the house of worship. He was a deacon in 1661, and it was said, "whatever the town had to do, Mr. Parker was likely to do it" [Hazen, GR., p. 104].

John married Mary (?Pope) Poulter Aylett who had been widowed twice. She had two children John Poulter (a founding father) and Elizabeth Poulter, who later married Jonathan Danforth. Mary had been briefly married to John Aylett @1639/40, and, during this period, John Parker had been Aylett's servant. John received 20 shillings from Aylett's will.

John Parker and Mary Aylett were married 23 June 1642 in Essex, England. John was 10 years her junior, having been born 4 June 1615 at Great Burstead, England.

The Billerica connections were strong in this family—not only with the Parkers, but also because Mary Aylett was the mother of John Poulter and Elizabeth (Poulter) Danforth.

'09,9,59

It is agreed by the major prt of the Towne, that there shall be a meeting house built this winter folling, thirty foote Longe and twenty and foure foot wide, and twelve foot high; the studs to be three foot asunder; the Committee apoynted to agree with workmen, to bild and finish the said house, are Ralph Hill, Sen'r, George Farley, Jonathan Danforth; it is agreed, also, that the sides and ends shall be covered with bords and the Roof with thatch."

Hazen, p. 154

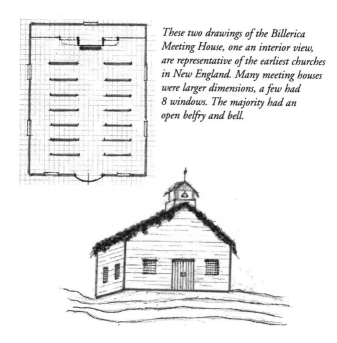

These two drawings of the Billerica Meeting House, one an interior view, are representative of the earliest churches in New England. Many meeting houses were larger dimensions, a few had 8 windows. The majority had an open belfry and bell.

Parker made a donation in 1657 to Harvard College on behalf of his brother James. In 1659, John was a recipient and overseer to the will of Edward Converse of Woburn, who called him "kinsman."

John died insolvent 14 June 1667 in Billerica with 68 creditors and debts of £568.03.02 [Middlesex Probate #16619]. His wife was allowed £50 from the estate.

Compared to most the inventory was quite colorful. In addition to household and barn items, Parker had 10 cows, a bull, two oxen, sheep, pigs and horses. In the house was "rumm" worth £4, wine 8s, bacon 6s, tobacco 6s, molasses £2, a bearskin and a moose skin. He also had considerable clothing.

In 1674, his widow Mary married for the fourth time to Thomas Chamberlaine of Chelmsford, MA. However, before she wed, Mary composed her will dated March 1673/4 [Middlesex Probate #16724]. Her son John Poulter was to have 20 shillings to be paid as a hat and shoes and what "I give him in my widowhood." She singled out her grandchild Anna Danforth to have a feather bed. The estate remainder was to go to her daughter Elizabeth Danforth. Son-in-law Jonathan Danforth was the executor.

Founding Father
ROBERT PARKER

m. -----, Judith (--------) Bugby, widow of Richard Bugby
    b. 1602, Essex, England
    d. 8 May 1682, Cambridge, MA

Children	Born	Married	Died
1. Benjamin	June 1636, Cambridge, MA	1661, Sarah Hartwell	17 Jan. 1671/2, Billerica, MA
2. Nathaniel	28 July 1638, Cambridge, MA	-----	Before 1659, -----
3. Sarah	Apr. 1640, Cambridge, MA	(1) 1662, Thomas Foster Son of a founding father (2) 1687, Peter Bracket A founding father	17 Apr. 1718, Roxbury, MA
4. John	bp. 27 Mar. 1642, Cambridge, MA	-----	1661-1685, -----
5. Rachell	c.1644, Cambridge, MA	-----	5 Apr. 1663, Cambridge, MA

Pioneers of Billerica • Settling the Shawshine Wilderness: 1654-1660

Robert Parker

b.	*1602/3, England*
emig.	*1633*
m.	*before 6 December 1635, Judith (-----) Bugbee, --------*
d.	*between 21 March & 7 April 1685, Cambridge, MA*

In February 1654/5, Robert Parker expressed a vital interest in Billerica when he was a signer of the petition to separate the area of Shawshine from Cambridge Township and call it Billerica. He acquired a tract in the Dudley Farm at this time, perhaps as a land speculator, for he chose to remain in Cambridge during his lifetime. In Billerica, Robert was a constable in 1656 and a fence viewer 1654/5.

Parker had acquired a half-acre plot in Cambridge in 1636, located on the Watertown side of the community. He sold two properties in Newtown, MA in 1637 and a six-acre plot in Cambridge's Old West Field. Designated a planter, Robert continued to buy and sell properties, some with houses and barns in Cambridge, MA on the south side of the Charles River for a period of 45 years.

Joseph Daniel, son of the deceased Robert Daniel, applied at the court on 7 April 1657 for guardianship under Robert Parker [Middlesex Co. Probate #5939].

On 24 November 1665 James Parker and Thomas Chamberlaine--now of Chelmsford, MA--sold Robert 125 acres in Billerica with 8 acres of meadow. On 4 April 1671, Jonathan Danforth bought 35 acres of this land from Judee and Robert Parker.

The remaining property in Billerica became the farm and residence of Robert's oldest son Benjamin. Benjamin also acquired a piece south of Bare Hill, on the east side of the Boston Road.

Robert Parker was born in England @1602/3 and came to America in 1633 as a servant to William Aspinall. Aspinall had arrived in Charlestown, MA in 1630, and returned to England in 1652. While in New England, Aspinall was described as abusive, argumentative and rigid—a very difficult personality.

Parker became a Freeman in Cambridge 1634/5.

Jugged Hare

A large heat-proof crock/cauldron to cook in a larger pan of boiling water deep enough to take the crock under itw own lid. It can be cooked outdoor in fair weather.

1 rabbit, cut into serving pieces
(the fork did not come into use for another hundred years)

salt and pepper
1 1/2 cups fine oatmeal
butter for frying
2 small onions, peeled and stuck with 4 whole cloves
1 large tart apple, slides
1 small lemon sliced
1/2 small whole mushrooms
1/2 teaspoon marjoram, dried
1/2 teaspoon thyme, dried
3 bay leaves
small bunch parsley, tied with string
1 cup red wine
2 cups beef stock
12 forcemeat balls
red currant jelly

Forcemeat balls:
1 1/2 cups raw veal or chicken, minced
one medium onion, chopped fine
1 teaspoon dried thyme
2 teaspoons chopped parsley
1/3 cup bread crumbs
1 beaten egg
salt, pepper, butter

Season rabbit and coat with oatmeal. Brown meat. Pack the rabbit into the crock. Mix wine and stock and pour in enough to fill the crock. Cover closely with lid or foil and stand in boiling water. Simmer for 3 hours. Near the end of the cooking time, make the forcemeat balls and brown in butter. Cook until done. Remove the rabbit when cooked to a serving dish and arrange forcemeat balls around. Make thin gravy of juices. Pour over rabbit. Serve very hot with toast and red currant jelly.

Before 6 December 1635, Robert married Judith (-----) Bugbee, the widow of Richard Bugbee, who had died between 1630 and 1632. The Bugbees had had two children and emigrated to New England with the Winthrop fleet to Roxbury, MA.

Robert and Judith had five children of their own. Their middle daughter married Thomas Foster, a son of the founding father, and after Thomas' death, a founding father, Peter Brackett.

Robert and Judith's marriage got off to a stormy start for on 6 December 1635, Robert was excommunicated from the Boston Church for "scandalous oppression of his wife's children in selling away their inheritance from them, and other hard usage both of her and them" [Boston Church Records, p.20]. Robert was received back into the church community 24 July 1636 after repentance.

Parker had a few difficulties with the civil authorities in Cambridge too, for felling two trees without permission and letting an ox feed in the cow common.

In Cambridge 8 May 1682, Judith Parker died, leaving Robert to be cared for by their daughter Sarah due to his infirmities. He had drafted a will 21 March 1684/5 which was probated 7 April 1685. Robert Parker died at the age of 82.

Robert's daughter Sarah Foster was the executrix of the will and benefited from the whole estate. When she died, Parker had wanted her son Thomas to have a double portion of the remaining estate. Robert stated he had already bestowed gifts to his deceased sons John and Benjamin. The inventory in 1685 totaled £197.16.0, £147 in real estate [Middlesex Probate #16783].

142

Founding Father
THOMAS PATTEN

m. (1) ——, Rebecca Paine, ——
    b. 19 Oct. 1642, Dedham, MA
    Daughter of Rebecca and Thomas Paine
    d. 19 May 1680, following childbirth, Billerica, MA

Children	Born	Married	Died
1. Mary	21 Aug. 1664, Billerica, MA	1702/3, Benjamin Cromwell	——, Charlestown, MA
2. Thomas	22 Mar. 1665/6, Billerica, MA	1699, Hannah Foster	14 Sept. 1752, Billerica, MA
3. Nathaniel	14 Sept. 1668, Billerica, MA	1695, Hannah Ross	2 Apr. 1718, Billerica, MA
4. William	12 May 1671, Billerica, MA	(1) ——, Mary Rogers	5 Oct. 1730, Cambridge, MA
		(2) ——, Elizabeth Whiting	
5. Rebeckah	29 Jan. 1674/5, Billerica, MA	1691, Joseph Davis	13 Feb. 1750/1, Billerica, MA
6. Sarah	8 June 1677, Billerica, MA		——
7. Elizabeth	8 May 1680, Billerica, MA	1701, James Wright	——, Medford, MA

Pioneers of Billerica • Settling the Shawshine Wilderness: 1654-1660

Thomas Patten

b.	*October 1636, Cambridge, MA*
m.	*(1) 1 April 1662, Rebecca Paine, --------*
	(2) 20 May 1686, Sarah (Kendall) Dutton, --------
d.	*16 January 1689/90, Billerica, MA*

Thomas Patten and his father William Patten were both founding fathers of Billerica. Thomas was born in Cambridge, MA in October 1636, either the first or second son of his parents. He grew up in Cambridge, but in 1654, acquired property and a house in Billerica just south of the Common at the central intersection of roads meeting there. He continued to acquire land during his lifetime. Using water of the Content Brook in "Pattenville," he set up a saw mill @1680. In the beginning, the mill was operated on a custom basis, but later expanded to greater production.

He was one of the town men who signed the Parker Agreement, allowing John Parker and Jonathan Danforth to have 1,000 acres each for setting out the metes and bounds for 2,000 acres granted by the General Court in 1681.

His large home was a garrison in 1675, a fortification for the families of Gouldin Moore, Samuel Frost, John Kidder, John Trull and Roger Toothaker. There were also seven soldiers to accommodate.

Thomas Patten married twice. His first wife was Rebecca Paine, whom he married 1 April 1662. They had seven children together.

Pioneers of Billerica • Settling the Shawshine Wilderness: 1654-1660

Founding Father
THOMAS PATTEN

m. (2) 20 May 1686, Sarah (Kendall) Dutton, ——
b. 22 June 1653, Reading, MA
Third marriage to Thomas Richardson
d. 20 Nov. 1734, ——

Children	Born	Married	Died
8. Mehittabel	28 Feb. 1686/7, Billerica, MA	——, William French	15 Jan. 1743, Billerica, MA
9. Kendall	20 Apr. 1689, Billerica, MA	(1) ——, Abigail ——	14 Dec. 1770, Tewksbury, MA
		(2) ——, Abigail Kittredge	
		(3) ——, Sarah Kittredge	

Pioneers of Billerica • Settling the Shawshine Wilderness: 1654-1660

Thomas married again to Sarah (Kendall) Dutton 20 May 1686. They had two children together, both toddlers when Patten died 10 March 1690 in Billerica. He left a will [Middlesex Pro. #17030] written 14 January 1689/90.

The Patten Homestead, still standing on Route 129 in Billerica.

He expressed his wish that his wife Sarah have the household furnishings and cattle she brought with her into the marriage. He also wanted her to have the "great brass kettle" and cobis------ she helped him purchase. She was also to be given £3 of silver for that which she lent him.

Sarah was to have use of one half the dwelling house and the barns, use of the orchard, fields and animals as long as she was his widow and as along as her children were minors. However, if she married, she was to have £20 from the estate.

He wanted young son Kindall to be a least 12 years old before the whole estate was divided among the children. The eldest son was to have a double portion, "ye 2nd Division" property. Nathaniel was to have the property at Loes Plaine. William and Kindall would receive portions from the homestead and the meadows. William Patten and his wife were to be joint executors, with his brother Nathaniel Patten, Capt. Ralph Hill and Lieut. Joseph Tompson available to resolve differences.

The inventory total of the estate was listed at £308.00.0, with debts outstanding of £15.30.06.

Sarah did marry again, on 29 December 1690 in Billerica. She married Thomas Richardson (1645-1721). She died in 1734.

Founding Father
WILLIAM PATTEN

m.   ----, Mary ----
   b. ----
   Emigrated age 4/5 to Cambridge, MA with parents.
   d. 20 Sept. 1673, ----

Children	Born	Married	Died
1. Mary	1632-4, England	1652, John Griggs	1674-92, Watertown, MA
2. William	-----	-----	bu. 22 Mar. 1645/6, ------
3. Thomas	Oct. 1636, Cambridge, MA	(1) 1662, Rebecca Paine	16 Jan. 1689/90, ------
		(2) 1686, Sarah Kendall	
4. Sarah	27 Jan. 1638, Cambridge, MA	1679, Jonas Woodward	24 Sept. 1677, Cambrige, MA
5. Nathaniel	Jan. 1639, Cambridge, MA		Jan. 1639, Cambridge, MA
6. Nathaniel	29 July 1643, Cambridge, MA	-----	12 June 1725, Cambridge, MA

William Patten

b.	*1600-1605, --------*
emig.	-----
m.	*1629-31, Mary --------, England*
d.	*10 December 1668, Cambridge, MA*

William Patten was in Cambridge, MA before 1635 with a wife Mary and at least one toddler. The Cambridge Town Records stated that on 13 March 1635, Patten could sustain 100 cattle on the "other" side of the river for a few months, presumably, the south side of the Charles River. William used his earmark on his cattle. This was a large herd acquired through a shipment from Europe, or perhaps purchased from a village like Newbury, MA, where cattle were raised for sale on the extensive salt meadows there.

The agreement with Cambridge Town was that he was to have £20 for the cattle— one half in money and the other in "coen" (corn?).

In 1638, Cambridge agreed that he would have a herd of three score cows (60) to maintain: i.e. to water, feed, take them to the meadow in the morning, bring them into the barn in the evening, milk, etc.

In 1649, the town appointed Patten and Andrew Steenenfon to care and tend hogs as

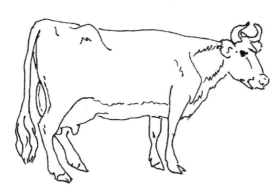

well as cattle. During this period in Cambridge, William's home place was on Massachusetts Avenue, opposite the Common. There was a note in the records stating that he was fined for felling trees on the Common without permission. In 1652, he had 90 acres of land.

Pioneers of Billerica • Settling the Shawshine Wilderness: 1654-1660

Pioneers of Billerica • Settling the Shawshine Wilderness: 1654-1660

Patten was granted an acre of land in Billerica 1654/5 for his house lot and seven acres adjoining the first lot along the Concord River, at the junction of the Boston and Floyd/Salem Roads.

Patten signed both the Cambridge Agreement in 1654/5 requesting that Billerica be a separate community from Cambridge, as well as the Whiting Agreement in 1658 giving the new minister his house and an income for his services.

William Patten died intestate in Cambridge 10 December 1668 at the age of 63-68 years old. The estate was divided 6 April 1669 between his widow Mary and the children: Thomas, Nathaniel, Sarah Patten and Mary Griggs [Middlesex Probate #17039]. The inventory lists few articles of clothing; it appears Patten had a modest lifestyle. Numerous animals were noted: pigs, six cows, one pair of oxen and four horses. Much of his land was sown in grain. The inventory total was £199.03.08.

His widow Mary was to have one-half the house and one-half the swamp, plus one-third part of the "movables" (i.e. furniture, household items, barn equipment, etc.). The remainder of the estate was to be divided with the children as noted.

Pioneers of Billerica • Settling the Shawshine Wilderness: 1654-1660

Founding Father

JAMES PATTISON

Probably a son of James Pattison

m. ———, Rebecca Stevenson, ———
b. 20 Jan. 1642, Cambridge, MA
Daughter of Andrew Stevenson
d. After 1701, Billerica, MA

Children	Born	Married	Died
1. Mary	22 Aug. 1666, Billerica, MA	———	———
2. James	28 Feb. 1668/9, Billerica, MA		3 Oct. 1677, Billerica, MA
3. Andrew	4 Apr. 1672, Billerica, MA	1697, Elizabeth Kebbe	At sea 1707, Charlestown, MA
4. John	8 Apr. 1675, Billerica, MA	1702, Joanna Hall	———
5. Joseph	1 June 1677/8, Billerica, MA	(1) 1701, Mary Goodnow	1736, Watertown, MA
		(2) ———, Mary———	
		(3) 1724, Rebecca Livermore	
6. Rebecca	18 July 1680, ———	———	———
7. James	13 Apr. 1683, ———		1737, ———
8. Jonathan	31 Feb. 1685/6, ———	———	———

Pioneers of Billerica • Settling the Shawshine Wilderness: 1654-1660

James Pattison (Paterson)

b.   @1633, Scotland
emig.   1652
m.   29 May 1662, Rebecca Stevenson, Cambridge, MA
d.   14 July 1701, Billerica, MA

James Pattison was a Scotsman, whose clan was a victim of inter-clan warfare in the Highlands of Scotland for years. With all the conflict in the glen and the need to be at home to help his family and relatives, it is unlikely he ever thought of emigrating to America. However, a series of tragic events led to this conclusion.

In the September of 1651, following young Charles II's coronation in Edinburgh, Scotland, Charles led his Royalist Army south into the center of England. This army was comprised particularly of "volunteers" who had been forced into the service by their lairds and chiefs to prove their allegiance to the king. Charles II's nation was threatened by Oliver Cromwell and the Covenators who, with their army, wanted to usurp the throne and later did so.

The Royalists were stopped at Worcester, England, by an army twice their size, exhausted and with few supplies. The battle that ensued was a terrible slaughter with 4,000 Scots dead and probably 10,000 captured [Rapaport's "Scots for Sale" NE HGS 2003. Winter, p. 30]. Charles II was very lucky to escape to France.

Cromwell's army finished off many of the captured army by forcing them on a 75-mile march to London. Many of the men were wounded, barefoot or even naked, and with no food to eat but what they could scrounge in the fields. Disease and dysentery ended the lives of many of these survivors.

The Council of State took their time to decide what to do with the prisoners and decided that many of them would be sent to America as indentured servants.

James Pattison was one of these soldiers. One can imagine not only the horrors he saw and experienced in the war and long march to London, but also the anger he felt toward Charles II, Cromwell, the Council of State and the people who probably shunned him.

Pioneers of Billerica • Settling the Shawshine Wilderness: 1654-1660

He lost his family, his health, his homeland, his security and liberty.

James was herded aboard a ship with 300 people packed in the tiny vessel. He arrived at Charlestown, MA May 1652. He must have had a resilient and sturdy body to have survived this additional ordeal. Indentured servants in New England normally worked to pay off their transportation in a few years and to acquire a small piece of land, tools and clothing at the end of the service. James worked out his service and acquired some hard cash too.

In 1658, Pattison acquired about 75 acres of land in Billerica. His house lot was a little larger than usual at 32 acres, and was in the middle of the village, lying between Boston Road and the Concord River.

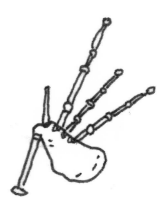

On 29 May 1662, James Pattison married Rebecca Stevenson, the older sister of Mary who married Thomas Richardson of Billerica. They were the daughters of Andrew Stevenson of Cambridge, the prison master.

This same year, James was convicted of provoking his wife and presumably abusing her with his great anger. He was unnaturally jealous of her. He had to pay a bond of £40, a very large sum, although Rebecca pleaded for the court to be lenient.

Their marriage improved and lasted nearly 40 years, with the birth of two daughters and six sons. His large home was a garrison during the Indian tensions for eight soldiers and four families, notably the Jefts, Farmers and Baldwins.

James Pattison died 13 July 1701 in Billerica "about 68" years old and left a will [#17047]. He signed this with a mark with his name spelled "Paterson" by the court scribes. Rebecca survived him in Billerica and was the executrix of his will. In the inventory value of £107.15.0, over £41 of this was to be paid out for debts.

Rebecca was to have full use of the estate for four years, then divide assets with the children who were not listed, except for Andrew, who was to have a double portion. His brother-in-law Andrew Stevenson, Capt. Joseph Tompson and Oliver Whiting were overseers to the will.

Founding Father

JOHN POULTER

Son of Mary (--------) and John Poulter of Raleigh, Essex, England.

m. (1) --------, Rachel Eliot, daughter of Mary (Saunders) and Francis Eliot of Braintree, MA.
    b. 26 Oct. 1643, Braintree, MA
    Her second marriage was to Deacon John Whitmore.
    d. 20 Mar. 1723, Medford, MA
    bu. at the Salem St. Cemetery in Medford, MA.

Children	Born	Married	Died
1. Elizabeth	c.1663, --------	1693, --------	------, Medford, MA
2. Mary	9 Apr. 1665, Billerica, MA	(1) 1687, Samuel Winship (2) 1701, Isaac Powers	2 Oct. 1745, Lexington, MA
3. John	23 Dec. 1666, Billerica, MA	1695, Hannah Hammond	22 June 1744, Lexington, MA
4. Jonathan	25 Jan. 1668/9, Billerica, MA	c.1692, Elizabeth(?) Coolidge	25 Aug. 1708, Lexington, MA
5. Rachel	14 Mar. 1670/1, Billerica, MA	c.1690, Thomas Brown	------, Concord, MA
6. Hanah	4 Mar. 1672, Billerica, MA	1697, John Dudley	20 Dec. 1707, Concord, MA Died in childbirth
7. Joseph	15 Feb. 1674/5, Billerica, MA	------	27 Mar. 1674/5, ------
8. Benoni, *twins*	18 Sept. 1676, Billerica, MA	------	12 Nov. 1696, Lexington, MA
9. Abiel, *twins*	18 Sept. 1676, Billerica, MA	------	6 Sept. 1757, Lexington, MA

Pioneers of Billerica • Settling the Shawshine Wilderness: 1654-1660

John Poulter

b.	*1635, Raleigh, Essex, England*
emig.	-----
m.	*29 December 1662, Rachel Eliot,--------*
d.	*18 September 1676, Medford, MA*

In 1657, at age 22, John Poulter moved to Billerica. His older sister Elizabeth had married Jonathan Danforth and moved to Shawshine in 1653/4 with their widowed mother Mary. John Poulter, Sr. had died in Raleigh, Essex, England and in his will bequeathed £50 to John and £100 to Elizabeth. With his legacy, John purchased an eight-acre property with a 29-acre house lot partly on the village, partly on the Common at Allen Street.

Poulter married 29 December 1662 Rachel Eliot with whom he had nine children. During the Indian Wars of 1675, the family fled Billerica to live in Medford, MA. Their son John bought 212 acres of land in Lexington, MA on the southeast side of Vine Street and south of the highway to include the Munroe Tavern property. Poulter Street in Lexington is a remembrance of this family's place in that community.

John Poulter died 18 September 1676 intestate in Medford, MA and was buried at the Old Bury Ground. Sons John and Jonathan sold the eight-acre Billerica property to Joseph Davis. On 2 May 1693, probably after their mother's death, Samuel and Mary (Poulter) Winship, Thomas and Rachel (Poulter) Brown, Hannah Poulter, Benoni Poulter and Elizabeth Poulter quit claimed their rights to the Billerica property to their two brothers for 10 shillings. For some reason, Abiel Poulter was not included in this transaction.

The inventory of John's estate indicated he was a man of substance with property in Billerica and Medford, MA and England, and had books and two Bibles.

Founding Father

JOHN ROGERS
Son of John Rogers, a Freeman in Watertown, MA 1637
m. (1) 1640, Priscilla Dawes from Boston, MA
    b. ------
    d. 21 Apr. 1663, Billerica, MA

Children	Born	Married	Died
1. John	11 Sept. 1641, ------	(1) 1667, Mary Shed	5 Aug. 1695, Billerica, MA
		(2) 1688/9, Abigail Rogers	Abigail wounded at John's death by Indians; 1 daughter scalped and survived; 2 children taken captive.
2. Mary	26 Oct. 1643, ------	1668, John French (a founding family)	16 June 1677, Billerica, MA
3. Thomas	c.1640, ------	(1) 1672, Hannah Shed	6 Aug. 1695, Billerica, MA
		(2) 1680/1, Mary Brown	He and son killed by Indians
4. Abigail	21 Jan. 1655, Watertown, MA	1667, Arthur Warren	15 June 1671, ------
5. Daniel	------, Billerica, MA	1686, Mary Russell	4 Feb. 1727/8, Billerica, MA
6. Nathaniel	------, Billerica, MA	1685, Martha Cloyes	3 Oct. 1730, Billerica, MA
7. Priscilla	------, Billerica, MA	1682, Simon Coolidge	1694, Watertown, MA
8. Francis	------, Billerica, MA	------	------

John Rogers

b.	*1611/2, England*
emig.	--------
m.	*(1) 1640, Priscilla Dawes, --------*
	(2) 6 July 1669, Elizabeth (--------) Brown, Billerica, MA
d.	*25 January 1685/6, Billerica, MA*
bu.	*Old South Bury Ground, Billerica, MA*

John Rogers achieved status as a Freeman in Watertown, MA in 1639, since he was a member in good standing in the community and church, and had acquired property. The following year (1640) he married Priscilla Dawes of Boston, MA as his first wife. They had eight children before she died 21 April 1663 in Billerica, MA.

Six years later, on 6 July 1669, John married the widow Elizabeth Brown. The two of them had three more daughters, all of whom died young.

In 1645, when John acquired a legacy, his occupation was said to be as a clothier. However, by 1660 in Billerica, he was the village baker. This community gave him several poles of land to butt the 23 acres he received in 1656 along the Concord Road as it split off from Boston Road. This extra land was to "set a kitchen-house" on. This occupation was confirmed in his daughter Abigail Warren's will.

Rogers acquired another house on the west side of Long Street.

John Rogers died 25 January 1685/6 in Billerica, an elderly man. He was buried in the Old South Bury Ground. He did not leave a will.

Many of John's 11 children had died previously. Two of his remaining sons John and Thomas were killed in 1695 in Indian warfare.

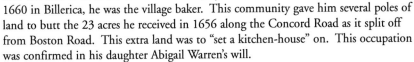

Founding Father

JOHN ROGERS

m. (2) 6 Jul. 1669, Elizabeth (--------) Brown from Boston, MA

b. -----

d. -----

Children	Born	Married	Died
9. Hannah	6 May 1670, Billerica, MA	-----	24 May 1670, Billerica, MA
10. Bethia	-----, Billerica, MA	-----	29 Dec. 1672, Billerica, MA
11. Sarah	-----, Billerica, MA		9 Jan. 1676/7, Billerica, MA

Pioneers of Billerica • Settling the Shawshine Wilderness: 1654-1660

Pioneers of Billerica • Settling the Shawshine Wilderness: 1654-1660

Founding Father
DANIEL SHEDD
Son of Daniel and Sarah Shed of Essex, England
m. (1) ----, Mary ?Gurney, ----
b. ----, Braintree, MA
d. 1658/9, ----

Children	Born	Married	Died
1. Mary	8 Mar. 1647, Braintree, MA	1667, John Rogers He was killed by Indians 1695	17 Aug. 1688, Billerica, MA
2. Daniel	30 Aug. 1649, Braintree, MA	1670, Ruth More	24 Oct. 1690, Billerica, MA Smallpox
3. Hannah	7 Sept. 1651, Braintree, MA	1672, Thomas Rogers	19 Dec. 1672, Billerica, MA
4. John	2 Mar. 1654, Braintree, MA Militia	1676/7, Sarah Chamberlin	31 Jan. 1736/7, Billerica, MA
5. Elizabeth, *twins*	17 June 1656, Braintree, MA	1677, Samuel Farley	----, Billerica, MA
6. Zechariah, *twins*	17 June 1656, Braintree, MA	(1) 1677/8, Anne Bray Killed by Indians with two children; house burnt down (2) 1692/3, Lydia Farley (3) 1702, Hannah Harris	May-July 1735, Chelmsford, MA
7. Sarah	30 Oct. 1658, Braintree, MA	1681, John Dutton	27 Feb. 1720/1, Billerica, MA

Daniel Shedd (Shed)

bp.   *25 June 1620, Finchingfield, Essex, England*
emig.   *@1643*
          (1) 1647/8, Mary ?Gurney Braintree, MA
          (2) 1659, Elizabeth ?Gurney, Billerica, MA
d.   *27 July 1708, Billerica, MA*

Daniel Shedd achieved recognition in Braintree/Quincy, MA between 1643 and 1658 before he settled in the village of Billerica. He arrived in New England about 1643 from Essex, England, when he was about 23 years old. He had no money, but he had ideas, a strong body and his faith.

In 1645, Shedd and 31 male residents of Braintree implored the General Court to initiate a plantation at Warwick, Rhode Island. This request was refused because the preacher of the colony-to-be Samuel Gorton was considered a heretic.

About 1646, Daniel leased a 100-acre tract in Braintree that had been granted to Rev. William Tompson. At that time, this area became known as Shed's Neck, Braintree. It is now Quincy, and is a peninsula of land in between Town River Bay and Quincy Bay, with the port Snug Harbor facing North Weymouth. His home was said to have been destroyed by fire.

In 1659 Shedd, Christopher Webb and Thomas Foster of Braintree elected to move away from the sea to begin a new life in Billerica. There may have

Pioneers of Billerica • Settling the Shawshine Wilderness: 1654-1660

Founding Father

DANIEL SHED (SHEDD)

m. (2) ——, Elizabeth ?Gurney, ——

b. ——

d. 17 Jan. 1699/1700, ——

Children	Born	Married	Died
8. Samuel	13 Aug. 1660, Billerica, MA	——, Elizabeth Bowers	——, Chelmsford, MA
9. Susan	29 Dec. 1662, Billerica, MA	(1) ——, William Hooper (2) 1693, Benjamin Dutton	——, Billerica, MA
10. Unice	19 Mar. 1664/5, Billerica, MA	1705, John Levistone	——, Chelmsford, MA
11. Nathan	5 Feb. 1668/9, Billerica, MA	1693/4, Mary French	18 June 1736, Billerica, MA

Pioneers of Billerica • Settling the Shawshine Wilderness: 1654-1660

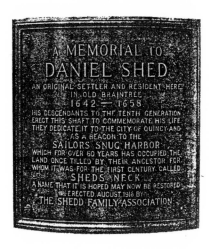

A MEMORIAL TO DANIEL SHED

AN ORIGINAL SETTLER AND RESIDENT HERE
IN OLD BRAINTREE
1642 — 1658
HIS DESCENDANTS TO THE TENTH GENERATION
ERECT THIS SHAFT TO COMMEMORATE HIS LIFE
THEY DEDICATE IT TO THE CITY OF QUINCY AND
AS A BEACON TO THE
SAILORS SNUG HARBOR
WHICH FOR OVER 60 YEARS HAS OCCUPIED THE
LAND ONCE TILLED BY THEIR ANCESTOR FOR
WHOM IT WAS FOR THE FIRST CENTURY CALLED
SHEDS NECK
A NAME THAT IT IS HOPED MAY NOW BE RESTORED
ERECTED AUGUST, 1916 BY
THE SHEDD FAMILY ASSOCIATION

been any number of reasons for Daniel's move, but he had recently remarried following his first wife's death.

Shedd purchased about 100 acres of land from George Willice, which had originally been granted to Joseph Parker. This 23-acre house lot was south of Boston Road, immediately west of the Concord Road at Charnstaffe.

In 1661, Shedd and 20-odd other Billerica residents agreed that John Parker and Jonathan Danforth should each have 1,000 acres of land, out of the 4,000 granted by the General Court, to survey and make available to the remainder to the Billerica community.

Between 1667 and 1675, the residents of the town became increasingly anxious about the Indian turmoil to their west, south and north. Rev. Whiting's house, next to Shedd's, was the main garrison during the flare-up of 1675/6.

Two of Daniel's sons Zachary and Daniel Shedd, Jr., built their residences north of Rogers Street near the falls. Zachary's wife Anne and two children were all murdered in the Indian attack of 1 August 1692. For some unexplained reason, Daniel Shedd's house was unharmed while the small community in North Billerica was devastated. Shedd's former son-in-law was killed in another attack in 1698.

Shedd had two wives, whose surnames may have been Gurney, who may have been related. His first wife was Mary -------- of Braintree, who was the mother of seven children after their marriage @1647/8. Mary died 1658/9 and, as was the custom, he remarried Elizabeth -------- promptly. She became the stepmother to his family and then had four children with him. One of his wives is thought to have been related to John Gurney whom Daniel called "father."

Daniel Shedd died in Billerica 27 July 1708. His second wife's death preceded his own 17 January 1699/1700.

Founding Father

JOHN SHELDON

Son of Isaac Sheldon of Dorchester, MA. Perhaps from Warwickshire, England. Sailed 1634 from Weymouth, England.

m. ----, Mary (Converse) Tompson of Woburn, MA.

    b. ----

        Widow of Simon Tompson who died in 1658.

    d. ----

Children	Born	Married	Died
1. John	24 Apr. 1660, Billerica, MA	1690, Deborah Hill	27 Aug. 1724, Billerica, MA
A deacon			

Pioneers of Billerica • Settling the Shawshine Wilderness: 1654-1660

John Sheldon

b.   *@1631, Warwickshire, England*
m.   *1 February 1658/9, Mary (Converse) Tompson, Woburn/Billerica,*
        MA
d.   *23 May 1690, Billerica, MA*

John, Isaac and William Sheldon were sons of Isaac Sheldon of Dorchester, MA. John and William moved to Billerica in 1658, where William planned to set up a corn mill within two years for the brothers to run. William acquired 44 acres on the side of Fox Hill, near the Common for this venture, but by 1663, the mill was still not built or running. The selectmen pressured the two brothers, who became very angry and complained of injustice and unfairness. John had signed both the Parker and Whiting Agreements about the allocation of land dispersal in 1658. However, with the town's criticism, John left to live in Woburn, MA a few years. His brother William moved east to Salem, MA for the rest of his life, and died there in 1691 at the age of 80. The third brother Isaac decided to move to new opportunities in Windsor, CT.

In March 1674, John Sheldon returned to Billerica. The town "considering the unquietness of his spirit, and being willing he should again returne to the towne" [Hazen, GR pp. 133-4], granted him 40 acres adjoining the land on Fox Hill. The town also defined that this should end the "difference" between William Sheldon and Billerica over mills and land divisions. John's house was southeast of the Andover Road near Pond Street.

In December 1675, John was one of 13 men from Woburn to join the militia for the Narragansett Expedition fighting King Philip and most of the Indian nation. The warriors, in small bands, assaulted towns from the Connecticut River to the north in Vermont/New Hampshire south into Massachusetts and Rhode Island. Over half of the English communities were attacked. In 1725, long after Sheldon had died, Massachusetts granted land to the servicemen of this expedition on property called the "Narragansett Grants." In 1691, Sheldon purchased six acres of upland next to his tract, which was bounded by the Commons. In this lot, "there is also allowance of one rod wide…to pass to the brick kilns with carts, etc…, though no open highway" [Hazen, GR, p. 134].

John Sheldon died 24 May 1690 in Billerica. He did not leave a will.

Pioneers of Billerica • Settling the Shawshine Wilderness: 1654-1660

Founding Father

JOHN STERNES

m. (1) 1653, Sarah Mixer of Watertown, MA

b. -----

d. 18 June 1656, Billerica, MA

Children	Born	Married	Died
1. John	2nd week of May 1654, Billerica, MA A Captain	(1) -----, Elizabeth Bigelow (2) -----, Johannse C. Parker	26 Oct. 1728, Billerica, MA

Pioneers of Billerica • Settling the Shawshine Wilderness: 1654-1660

John Sternes (Stearns)

b.   *1630, possibly in England or aboard ship to America*
emig.   *1630 on the ship "Arabella"*
m.   *(1) 1653, Sarah Mixer, Watertown, MA*
         (2) 20 November 1656, Mary Lathrop, Barnstable, MA
d.   *5 March 1668/9, Billerica, MA*

At the age of 22, John Sternes left the family home in Watertown, MA, where his father was a tailor, selectman, surveyor for highways, constable and owner of considerable property. John elected to move to the Shawshine Wilderness in 1654, and bought 50 acres of land on the northeast corner of Dudley Farm and another 50 acres on the Concord River. His home was on the south side of Charnstaffe Lane. John acquired another parcel of land west of the Concord Road in 1660, and an island of upland on the west side of the Concord River.

The home of John Sternes on Dudley Road in Billerica.

Sternes was one of the signers of the request to the Cambridge authorities in 1654 for Shawshine to secede from Cambridge and be called Billerica.

John was primarily a farmer with land next to the Reverend Whiting's home. The Selectmen, in protection of the minister's valuable time, admonished Sternes to keep his cattle and swine secure.

John was the son of Mary and Isaac Sternes, who migrated in 1630 from Neyland with Wissington, Suffolk, England. They sailed on the ship "Arabella" to Salem, MA. It is believed John was born in 1630, possibly enroute to America or possibly in England.

Pioneers of Billerica • Settling the Shawshine Wilderness: 1654-1660

Founding Father

JOHN STERNES

m. (2) 20 Nov. 1656, Mary Lathrop, Barnstable, MA

b. 4 Oct. 1640, Barnstable, MA

She later married Capt. William French 1669 (4 children) and Isaac Mixer.

d. After 1735

Children	Born	Married	Died
2. Isaac	17 Apr. 1658, Billerica, MA	-----	9 Oct. 1659, Billerica, MA
3. Samuel	3 Sept. 1659, Billerica, MA	-----	1735, Billerica, MA
		Disabled	
4. Isaac	23 Dec. 1661, Billerica, MA	-----, Mary Meriam	1739, Billerica, MA
5. Nathaniel	30 Nov. 1663, Billerica, MA	-----	After 1685, but young, -----
6. Thomas	6 Dec. 1665, Billerica, MA	1688, Rebecca Chamberlaine	9 Feb. 1696/7, Billerica, MA

Pioneers of Billerica • Settling the Shawshine Wilderness: 1654-1660

About the time of his move to Billerica, John married Sarah Mixer of Watertown, the daughter of Sarah and Isaac Mixer. When her father died, Isaac Mixer bequeathed Sarah one half of his vessel the "Diligent" with a value of £100 [Middlesex Co. #15301].

Sarah Sternes died 14 June 1656, the second person to die in Billerica, MA. She may have died in childbirth. She and John had one son John, Jr. in May 1654.

John Sternes remarried a few months later: 20 November 1656 to Mary Lathrop of Barnstable, MA. She was the daughter of Mary (Learned) and Thomas Lathrop. John and Mary had five children together.

John was the town clerk of Billerica for two years and constable in 1658.

He died 5 March 1668, probably unexpectedly, for he did not leave a will. He left five minor children. The second oldest child Samuel was disabled and needed care for the rest of his life.

An inventory was made of John Sternes' estate. He had 315 acres of upland and 33 acres of meadow. He had farm and wood cutting equipment and animals: four oxen, ten cows, two horses and four pigs. His home was called a Sill home, which seems to have been one built with a threshold for the door rather than on ground level. The house had a cellar, parlor, hall (bed)chambers and a cooking kitchen. The estate was valued at £390.18.04. with debts of £52.05.1/2 [Middlesex Pro. #21259].

John Sternes' gravestone at the Old South Burying Ground.

Pioneers of Billerica • Settling the Shawshine Wilderness: 1654-1660

Founding Father

WILLIAM TAY (TOY, TOO, TOUW)

m. ——, Grace Newell, daughter of Abraham Newell
b. 1621, Roxbury, MA
d. 11 April 1712, Roxbury, MA

Children	Born	Married	Died
1. Grace	23 Aug. 1645, ——	1662/3, Thomas Willice	23 Jan. 1716, Medford, MA
2. John	16 Nov. 1647, ——	c.1670/2, Elizabeth Gannett	1678, Billerica, MA
3. Isaiah	4 Mar. 1651, ——	——	after 1683, Boston, MA
4. Abiel	21 Jan. 1652, ——	——	——
5. Nathaniel	23 Feb. 1654, ——	1677, Barsheba Wyman	18 Apr. 1724, Woburn, MA
6. Jeremiah	18 July 1657, ——	1683, Mercy Woodward	——, Boston, MA
7. Elizabeth	25 June 1660, ?Billerica, MA	——	before 1680, ——

William Tay (Toy, Too, Touw)

b.   1608, England
m.   17 September 1644, Grace Newell, Roxbury, MA
d.   [will] 12 April 1683, Boston, MA

William Tay was admitted to the Puritan Church in Boston, MA in 1642. In 1644, Tay married Grace Newell of Roxbury, a marriage that lasted 40 years. William and Grace had seven children together, probably most of them born in Boston.

Tay made his living in Boston as a distiller of "strong water" or liquors by condensing the vapors from grain mash and fruit spirits. It was a profitable business, especially after molasses from the West Indies was brought in to make rum – a very favorite tipple.

On leaving England, William first emigrated to New Netherlands (New York), where he acquired some property on Long Island. It may be that he did not feel at home with the primarily Dutch culture of this area, which was more varied and loose than Boston. The church services too were very different, especially since they were conducted in Dutch. It is also possible there was more competition from other breweries and distilleries which flourished in New York, for there was a tavern on every corner in that city.

Tay exchanged his two-acre property on Long Island with Leonard Buttels for 20 acres on Muddy River, now identified as Olmstead Park, Boston.

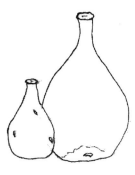

In November 1656, William was granted a single share of land or 120 acres in Billerica, although he did not acquire this property for two years. The land was partly by the Commons, west of Bare Hill. It was upland, bound by Boston Road.

Tay sold his Boston property 6 October 1663. In 1664, he was the town clerk of Billerica, but in 1675, he and his family fled to their former city for protection from the Indians.

Pioneers of Billerica • Settling the Shawshine Wilderness: 1654-1660

Pioneers of Billerica • Settling the Shawshine Wilderness: 1654-1660

William Tay died in Suffolk County and left a will 12 April 1683. His wife Grace died in Roxbury 11 April 1712 at 91 years of age.

Tay's will was proven 12 April 1682 (written 28 April 1680) [Suffolk County, Vol. 4:289]. His wife was the sole executor. He gave his son Jeremiah and daughter Elizabeth the property "that the house was burnt on" in the fire of 1679.

Tay's granddaughter Elizabeth (daughter of son John) was to have £10 when she was 18 or married. He bequeathed housing to Nathaniel, to Grace Meade of Billerica ("whose husband is not of my acquaintance") and to son Isaiah.

Pioneers of Billerica • Settling the Shawshine Wilderness: 1654-1660

Founding Father

JOSEPH TOMPSON
Son of Rev. William Tompson, minister of the Braintree, MA congregation

m. (1) ——, Mary Bracket, ——
   b. 12 May 1641, Braintree, MA
      Daughter of Richard and Alice (Blower) Bracket
   d. 23 Mar. 1678/9, Billerica, MA

Children	Born	Married	Died
1. Mary	18 Nov. 1663, Braintree, MA	——	dy
2. Joseph	8 Apr. 1666, Billerica, MA		Before 1732
3. Abigail	16 Apr. 1667, Billerica, MA	(1) 1701, John Watkins (2) ?Joshua Scottow	After father, Charlestown, MA
4. William B.	3 Oct. 1670, Billerica, MA	——	22 Dec. 1694, Billerica, MA
5. Deborah	29 Sept. 1676, Billerica, MA	?1701, John Hartwell	1744, Concord/Bedford, MA

Joseph Tompson (signature)

★

Joseph Tompson, Captain

b.	*1 May 1640, Braintree, MA*
m.	*(1) 22 July 1662, Mary Bracket, Billerica, MA*
	(2) 17 March 1680/1, Mary Denison, Billerica, MA
d.	*13 October 1732, --------*

Joseph Tompson was 20 years old when he located in Billerica in 1660. He acquired land in the southeast part of the village, on a small section of the Dudley Farm as it stretched into Loes Plain, north of Boston Road. He took as his first wife Mary Bracket, the sister of John and Peter Bracket, founding fathers. The couple married 22 July 1662 in Billerica.

Joseph had received an education, and with his learning and skills, became the first Billerica schoolmaster beginning 1679/80. Some children in Billerica started school at the age of four years. It was a very long day for the youngster—whether 4 or 16 years old—since there were fires to be set in the kitchen at home by dawn and animals to be fed before school began. A boy would additionally need to be sure the wood box was filled for the day's use and chop a little more if it was insufficient. Girls were required to help their mother in the kitchen and tend to the babies with their nappies.

We cannot know how kindly Tompson was as a schoolmaster, but the early New England teacher was autocratic, harsh and quick to punish with a stick and humiliation. He would have expected the children to learn by memorization and cipher and to acquire beautiful penmanship. Boys and girls made their own copybooks out of paper they could acquire in the home and even made their own ink and quill pens. Teachers were not required to teach the children all the skills they needed for their life. Fathers would teach their sons the needed skills for finances, care of the animals, husbandry, hunting and fishing. Mothers and some special lady in the village might teach their daughters to embroider samplers with their ABC's and names, and to acquire special skills spinning and weaving cloth.

Joseph was a town clerk for years, succeeding Jonathan Danforth. He was a selectman, and acquired stature as a representative to the Massachusetts Governing Body for

Founding Father

JOSEPH TOMPSON

m. (2) ----, Mary Denison, ----
       b. 1653, ----
       Daughter of Edward Denison of Roxbury, MA
       d. 9 Oct. 1743, ----

Children	Born	Married	Died
6. Edward	18 Jan. 1683/4, Billerica, MA	----	Before father 1732, ----
7. Benjamin	7 Feb. 1685, Billerica, MA	----	28 Oct. 1753, Billerica, MA
8. Elizabeth	29 June 1686, Billerica, MA		24 Aug. 1712, Boston, MA
9. Mary	17 Nov. 1691, Billerica, MA	1710, Ephraim Manning	After 1732, ----

Pioneers of Billerica • Settling the Shawshine Wilderness: 1654-1660

many years. He was a deacon in the Billerica church. Joseph also commanded the militia as Captain.

About 1675, the towns of Concord and Chelmsford wanted to wrest more land from the township of Billerica. In 1698, Joseph Tompson and a group of four petitioned the court to settle this dispute. Cambridge Court chose a committee to settle the disputed boundary lines. Billerica's claim to a tract of land between Concord and Chelmsford, west of the Concord River, was accepted.

His wife Mary Bracket died 23 March 1678/9. His second wife was Mary Denison of Roxbury, MA, whom he married 17 March 1680/1. Joseph had nine children between his two wives, five daughters and four sons.

He left a will in Billerica [Mdsx. Pro. #22485], probated after his death 13 October 1732. He willed all his personal and real estate to his son Benjamin. His widow Mary was to have use of the parlor in the home. In addition, Mary was to annually receive eight bushels of Indian corn, three bushels of rye, one bushel of wheat, two bushels of mault, 90 weight of young poultry, four barrels of cider, firewood and two milk cows. She was to receive £30 of money. His three daughters were noted with his youngest daughter Mary Manning already having received her portion of the estate with a previous gift of £160.

Abigail Scottow and Deborah Hartwell were each to have £30, and share equally two lots: one of 24 acres of meadow land and the other 36 acres of the upland mill lot. An additional sum of 20 shillings was to be given to each by the executor and son Benjamin from the sale of six small parcels of the mill lot. Abigail was also to receive 40 shillings from a legacy given to her by Grandmother Bracket.

Mary (Denison) died 9 October 1743 in Billerica.

Pioneers of Billerica • Settling the Shawshine Wilderness: 1654-1660

Once the home of Joseph Tompson, this center-chimney colonial stood near Tufts Lane.
(Courtesy of the Billerica Museum)

Pioneers of Billerica • Settling the Shawshine Wilderness: 1654-1660

Founding Father

ROGER TOOTHAKER

Son of Margaret and Roger Toothaker; stepfather Ralph Hill, Sr.

m. (1) ----, Mary Allin, daughter of Faith (Ingalls) and Andrew Allin
    b. c.1644, Andover, MA
    d. 5 Aug. 1695, Billerica, MA

Children	Born	Married	Died
1. Nathaniel	7 Apr. 1666, Billerica, MA	----	18 May 1682, Billerica, MA
2. Martha	23 July 1668, Billerica, MA	1690, Joseph Emerson	14 Jan. 1725/6, Haverhill, MA
3. Allin	17 July 1670, Billerica, MA	----	After 1692, Merrimack, NH
	Testified at Salem Trials		
4. Roger	27 Nov. 1672, Billerica, MA	(1) 1703, Sarah Rogers	9 Mar. 1745/6, Billerica, MA
		(2) 1718, Phebe Baldwin	
		(3) ----, Mary Richardson	
5. Sarah	1674, Billerica, MA	15 Nov. 1694, Jonathan Whitaker	----, Chelmsford, MA
	Indentured for foster care		
6. Mary	7 June 1675, Billerica, MA	----	14 Oct. 1675, Billerica, MA
7. Mary	28 Sept. 1676, Billerica, MA	----	5 Dec. 1683, Billerica, MA
8. Andrew	4 Oct. 1679, Billerica, MA	1707, Abigail (?White)	1760, Harpswell, ME
9. Margaret	31 Jan. 1682/3, Billerica, MA		----
	Captured by Indians	b. 5 Aug. 1695	

Roger Toothaker, Doctor

b.	*1634, England*
emig.	*September 1635 on the ship "Hopewell"*
m.	*9 June 1665, Mary Allin, --------*
d.	*16 June 1692, Boston, MA*

Roger Toothaker was one year old when he arrived in Plymouth, MA in September 1635 with his parents Margaret, age 28 and Roger, age 23. There were 51 other passengers on the ship "Hopewell." A Toothaker descendant, Margaret I. Gregory stated that the family's original surname was Whitaker, which had been changed to Toothaker because of religious persecution and for Roger, Sr. to avoid being drafted into the army.

Roger's father soon acquired property north of Plymouth, MA at Wellingland, Woburn Plains. He died about 1636, leaving Margaret with property and two children: Roger, Jr. and Martha. Two years later, Margaret married Ralph Hill, Sr. of Plymouth, MA, a founding father of Billerica, MA. Margaret's daughter Martha later married Ralph Hill, Jr., another founding father.

At age 19, young Roger Toothaker resided at Charlestown, MA. In 1654, he was employed as a servant for Samuel Eldred in Malden, MA, a community north of Boston center. In 1660, he moved to Billerica when his stepfather Ralph Hill, Sr. gave him a lot, which was located in North Billerica in the great common field on the east side of the Concord River, below the bridge. A future locator would be at the point where the Middlesex Canal left the Concord River.

Roger built a home there, which became one of the most northern houses in Billerica, MA. In 1664, he traded five acres of this tract, west of the road, for 12 acres of meadow, perhaps thinking of a future placement of a mill.

Roger went to court in 1673 accusing Thomas Martin of Cambridge, MA of abusing him.

Toothaker was a farmer, logger, hunter, as most of the men in town were to some degree, but he also practiced folk medicine. He did not have a degree or medical training, but depended on a number of ideas and treatments which fascinated him, such as herbal remedies, sorcery with the control of evil spirits, counter-magic, telling the present or future with the 12 signs of the zodiac, and isolated interpretations of the Bible in terms of good and evil, i.e. God and the Devil. The assumptions he made and conclusions drawn had little relation to rationality. He said his specialty was the detection and punishment of malevolence.

One must remember that in the 17th century, there had not been an awakening to rational or scientific thinking in the world. It was a fundamental universe, with the Holy Bible the basis for all Christian religious and political beliefs. An event that was awry, or an unnatural occurrence, created tremendous anxiety within the community. Epidemics, comets, shooting stars, deaths of babies, mental upsets, miscarriages, etc. were often interpreted as God's punishment for misdeeds or perhaps maliciousness from a neighbor's gossip. This thinking was not based on good common sense as we think of it today. Rigid religious standards escalated people's fears about their own faith and the faith of their neighbors. With survival at a high cost in the new world, community solidarity and loyalty to common values was at a premium. The churches too often added to the anxieties by preaching of hellfire and brimstone, and claimed that adversity was a result of one's sins.

Roger's extended family illuminates his own story. Roger Toothaker's wife was Mary Allin, one of the daughters of Faith (Ingalls) and Andrew Allin. Her sister was Martha (Allin) Carrier, who was married to Welshman Thomas Carrier, alias Morgan. He was born in 1626, and seems to have served in the Royal Army of England. Because of his easily identifiable over-seven-foot height and service history, he has traditionally been thought to have been one of the men who beheaded Charles I of England 30 January 1649.

Thomas emigrated to Cambridge, MA in 1635, married Martha and had six children. The family were considered outsiders, for they did not have status, assets or property. They found New Englanders cold and unfriendly, but the townspeople saw Martha as outspoken and unpleasant in her remarks, and they may have also felt alarmed by Thomas very large stature.

In 1676, the selectmen in Billerica raised many questions about admitting the Carriers to their town, for the Carriers did not appear to have income and there was illness in the family. Billerica could not assume the care and welfare of these people, so the selectman gave the family notice to leave in a few days, or they would have to pay 20 shillings a week as a pledge of security. They may have left and gone to Andover, MA for a time, but were back in Billerica in 1677, when Thomas Morgan cut brush on the south side of town.

In October 1690, Martha and Mary's father died in Andover, and the Carriers moved there to take care of their elderly widowed mother. The Andover selectmen also had

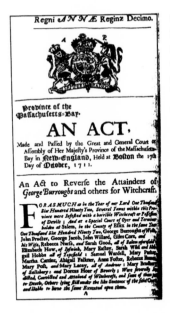

Regni *ANNÆ* Reginæ Decimo.

**Province of the
Massachusetts-Bay.**

AN ACT,

Made and Passed by the Great and General Court or
Assembly of Her Majesty's Province of the Massachusetts
Bay in New-England, Held at Bolton the 17th
Day of October, 1711.

An Act to Reverse the Attainders of
George Burroughs and others for Witchcraft.

FORASMUCH as in the Year of our Lord One Thousand
Six Hundred Ninety Two, Several Towns within this Province were Infested with a horrible Witchcraft or Possession
of Devils ; And at a Special Court of Oyer and Terminer
holden at Salem, in the County of Essex in the same Year
One Thousand Six Hundred Ninety Two, George Burroughs of Wells,
John Procter, George Jacob, John Willard, Giles Core, and
his Wife, Rebecca Nurse, and Sarah Good, all of Salem aforesaid ;
Elizabeth How, of Ipswich, Mary Estey, Sarah Wild and Abigail Hobbs all of Topsfield ; Samuel Wardell, Mary Parker,
Martha Carrier, Abigail Falkner, Anne Foster, Rebecca Eames
Mary Post, and Mary Lacey, all of Andover ; Mary Bradbury
of Salisbury ; and Dorcas Hoar of Beverly ; Were Severally In-
dicted, Convicted and Attainted of Witchcraft, and some of them
by Death, Others lying Bill under the Sentence of the false Con-
and liable to have the same Executed upon them.

serious reservations about the Carriers, especially since there was smallpox raging in the family. Within two months, nine people died in Andover from the pox: two of them Carriers. Thomas and Martha were accused of bringing disease into the village with "wicked callousness." The fact that Thomas and some of the children survived was suspect and this suspicion meant that Martha had magical powers.

Martha compounded her strained relationship with the Andover people when she settled her father's estate and caused friction with her sharp tongue. Andover wanted them out of town, but Salem did not want to admit them either.

On 28 May 1692, with a number of others, Martha Carrier was accused of being a witch. The hysteria of the Salem girls and women was out of control and for some unexplained reason Martha was blamed for Joseph Ballard's wife becoming ill.

In early testimony, Roger and Mary Toothaker's son Allin (Martha's nephew) age 22, testified that he had lost three cows because of his aunt's evil influences. When Allin fought with his 18 year old cousin Richard Carrier (Martha's son), Richard pulled Allin down to the ground by the hair on his head. When Allin got up, he planned to hit his cousin, but was unable to move until he saw his "Aunt Martha's shape leave his breast" [Salem Witchcraft, Vol. I, p. 242-3].

Martha also had told Allin that he would never be cured of the wounds he suffered in the wars. However, it was revealed that when Martha was arrested, he got well.

John Rogers of Billerica testified that when Martha threatened his cattle, they were bewitched.

To add to the vituperation against Martha, her brother-in-law Roger Toothaker gave evidence according to Hazen "too filthy for quotation" [p. 197]. There is no explanation for this remark in the witchcraft records.

Martha was called a "rampant hag" [Salem Witchcraft, Vol. I. P. 209-214]. The "Devil had promised her that she should be Queen of Hell." She was a woman who spoke her mind, regardless of the case she brought against herself, and claimed before the jury that there was a monstrous struggle going on between God and Evil.

During the trial, Phebe Chandler testified she heard Martha Carrier's voice "as if it were over her head." The voice said she should be poisoned in two to three days. Phebe claimed her head and face were already swollen [Salem Witchcraft, p. 186, Fowler].

A FAITHFUL

Warning & Exhortation
T O
FRIENDS
To Beware of
Seduc. g Spirits,

And to keep on the Armour of Light, in Sincerity and Simplicity, as their best Armour in all

TRYALS

Written by a Lover of Sincerity, and Traveller for Sion's Redemption, and for the Removing of all Oppressions from off the Souls of them who have believed,
STEPHEN CRISP.

Reprinted and Sold by *William Bradford* at *Philadelphia* in *Pennsylvania*, in the Year 1 6 9 2.

JANUARY hath 31 Days.

New Moon 8 day. 50 min. past 4 Morn.
First quart. 16 day 54 min. past 9 Morn.
Full Moon 23 day 34 min. past 9 Morn.
Last quart. 30 day 31 min. past Morn.

M. W.	Sur. Tides & Weather	Moons place
1 6	Sun r. 25 min. after 7	Scorpio
2 7	Sun sets 35 min. after. 4	
3 C		
4 2	cold Weather	Sagita
5 3		
6 4	Sun rise 23 min. after 7	Capric
7 5	Sun sets 37 min. after 4.	
8 6	Lun. in wet sign	Aquari
9 7		
10 C	Snow or cold Rain	Moon
11 2	Sun rise 18 min. afte 7	Pisces
12 3	Sun Sets 42 min after 4	
13 4		Aries
14 5	Lun. in cold sign	
15 6	cold and windy	
16 7	Sun rise 13 min. after 7	Taurus
17 C	Sun sets 47 min. after 4	
18 2	Snow or Hail	Gemini
19 3		
20 4	Spring Tides rise	Cancer
21 5	Sun rise 9 min. after 7	
22 6	Sun sets 51 min. after 4	Leo
23 7	High Tides	Moon
24 C	Sun rise 1 min. after 7	Virgo Moon
25 2	Sun sets 59 min. after 4	pereges
26 3	C Court at Boston	Libra
27 4	very cold	
28 5	Moon in wet sign	Scorpio Moon
29 6		
30 7	very Raw cold	
31 C		Sagit

Boston, H.B., Boston Almanac, 1692

Pioneers of Billerica • Settling the Shawshine Wilderness: 1654-1660

Benjamin Abbott testified that Martha Carrier caused him to have boils that did not heal until Martha herself was on trial.

Every idle rumor or fantastic idea that came to the minds of the Salem-Andover-Billerica townspeople was brought to bear against Martha. Roger Toothaker was clearly fascinated by all the ideas of counter-magic, as was his son Allin. However, Roger lived apart from his wife Mary, who was living on the town's aid in North Billerica, and was also alleged to be a witch. Mary (Allin) Toothaker was arrested May 1692 and taken to prison with Margaret Scot, ?Benjamin Abbott, Elizabeth J. Howe, M. Andrews, and her son Allin and husband Roger for their witchcraft. John Bradstreet of Andover was charged with bewitching a dog, but somehow Bradstreet avoided prison time. Nevertheless the dog was hung.

We also know that John Durrant and Rebecca Shelley Chamberlaine were imprisoned at this time.

When Martha was arrested 2 August 1692, four of their children were placed in prison with her. The youngest daughter Sarah, age 8 was put into "foster" care, and was then asked how long she, herself, had been a witch. Sarah knew she was a witch because a cat had told her so, and her mother came to her like a black cat. She spoke of her "Aunt Toothaker (Mary) as being a known witch. Two of her brothers Richard and Andrew (ages 18 and 15) denied knowing about this, but were tortured to make claims against their mother. The boys "confessed" after they were hung, tied neck to heel until blood spouted from their noses and mouths.

The Massachusetts Colony law was very clear in defining that a witch who consulted with a familiar spirit had to be punished by death. Martha Carrier was executed on Gallows Hill in Salem 19 August 1692. Over 200 people were accused of witchcraft at this time; 23 of them condemned to death by hanging, tortured or died in jail. Curiously, it has also been stated that during the trials, many people had seizures that at the time were considered a reflection of the witch's powers. There is some suspicion the wheat used for bread in Salem had poisonous properties.

After Martha's death, Thomas Carrier resumed his Morgan identity as Morgan ap Carrier. He moved to Colchester, CT and died there 18 May 1735. He was a virile fellow right to the end when he died at the age of 109 years.

The Roger and Mary (Allin) Toothaker story is also a tragedy. As stated, Martha (Allin) Carrier was accused of witchcraft in May 1692. Roger and his son Allin were at the trials and added detrimental testimony about Aunt Martha. Roger testified that he dealt in counter-magic in Salem where he resided and was referred to as Doctor. However, Roger's wife Mary was also charged as a witch, as was their daughter Martha Toothaker Emerson.

Noticeable problems began for Roger, when in May 1692, he boasted to Thomas Gage that his daughter Martha had killed a witch, for he had told her how to do it.

Pioneers of Billerica • Settling the Shawshine Wilderness: 1654-1660

Martha had acquired some of the "witches" urine and put it in an earthen pot, corked the opening, and placed this in a hot oven. The next morning the witch was dead— "bewitched to death." As with the fear of voodoo and its power, it is possible that the woman died (or as the court said, was murdered by witchcraft) knowing that her urine had boiled away.

The scene of the Witch Trials, the Jonathan Corwin house.

In his testimony in May, Roger spoke of others in Salem who used witchcraft on the bodies of Elizabeth Hubert, Ann Putnam and Mary Walcot. He confided that when he was living in Beverly, MA, one child he knew had fits, and the other was strangely sick. His conclusion as a Doctor was: they were "under an evil hand." While in Salem, he was accused of witchcraft surrounding a birth he attended.

Roger was transferred to the Boston prison on 18 May 1692 and died there 16 June 1692. The coroner and his team of 15 testified that he died in the jail at Boston by natural causes. However, it is believed that he had been tortured. "Dr. Roger Toothaker folk healer, self styled killer of witches, now a suspect, died in Boston jail" [Suffolk County Court Records, Vol. 32 #2690].

In the middle of June 1692, Mary (Allin) Toothaker learned that she was now a widow and again without financial support from her separated husband for the three minor children.

On trial from July to January 1692/3, Mary claimed that in the previous May (when the witchcraft-related anxieties were very high over Roger and her sister), she was very nervous, having nightmares and fearing that Indians would come to fight her. This was not an ill-based anxiety for there had been small, but repeated Indian alarms and attacks. She prayed, but the Devil had tempted her not to pray, and she now felt that her faith and baptism had not helped or reassured her. She said she had been a sinner for at least two years, when she had asked for the Devil's help. The Devil promised her that others would not discover her sin of asking for his help.

The Devil (whom she described was in the shape of a tawny man) told her that if she served him, she would be safe from the Indians, and made a mark with her finger on a piece of birch bark. She knew she was a witch and shared incidents from her life experiences were she had hurt people. She also said she was innocent, for it was the fear of the Indians that drove her to this behavior [Suffolk Court Record #2713].

Pioneers of Billerica • Settling the Shawshine Wilderness: 1654-1660

Mary related how Roger had instructed their daughter Martha in the use of witchcraft to kill Button, a reputed witch.

The Toothaker's daughter Martha Emerson, age 24, wife of Joseph Emerson for two years, was arrested 22 July 1692 for hurting Mary Warren and Mary Lacy. When the trial court reminded her that her father had taught her to use evil magic, "she confessed all." She stated she was innocent, but was jailed with her mother in the Cambridge prison for months.

On 1 August 1692, the embittered Indians of the area attacked Billerica, with at least six people slain. They came back a few days later to do more damage and burned out the deserted Toothaker home at the north edge of town.

On 1 February 1693, Martha and her mother were finally freed from their imprisonment. Martha Emerson went home to her husband in Haverhill. Young Roger Toothaker, age 21, was about to become a doctor, and daughter Sarah, age 19, lived with another family. Sarah married Jonathan Whitaker the following year (November 1694). Allin Toothaker moved to Merrimack, New Hampshire and had a family.

Mary Toothaker returned to the shell of her home in North Billerica to live with her younger children Andrew, 13, and Margaret, 11.

The Toothaker-Rogers house, still standing in North Billerica, Massachusetts. The gambrel-roofed ell on the left was the scene of the Indian attack of 1695.

On 5 August 1695, Mary's fears were realized, for the Indians returned to Billerica. She saw mounted men in the neighborhood, but did not seem to realize they were Indians on a mission to cause havoc and kill white settlers. The marauders killed 15 people that day, including Mary (Allin) Toothaker. The youngest daughter Margaret was taken captive and never seen again.

Pioneers of Billerica • Settling the Shawshine Wilderness: 1654-1660

Founding Father

JOHN TRULL   m.   ----, Sarah French, daughter of John French
b. Oct. 1637, Cambridge, MA
d. 26 Sept. 1710, ----

Children	Born	Married	Died
1. John	13 Jan. 1658, Billerica, MA	-----	1 Feb. 1658/9, Billerica, MA
2. Samuel	3 Sept. 1659, Billerica, MA	-----	died young, Billerica, MA
3. Sarah	27 May 1660, Billerica, MA		------
4. Mary	22 July 1662, Billerica, MA	1684, Benjamin Parker	15 Sept. 1694, Billerica, MA
5. John	19 May 1665, Billerica, MA	-----	22 June 1665, Billerica, MA
6. Elizabeth	31 May 1668, Billerica, MA	-----	11 July 1668, Billerica, MA
7. John	13 July 1669, Billerica, MA	1692, Elizabeth Hooper	----, Billerica, MA
8. Hannah	15 Oct. 1671, Billerica, MA	1693, James Frost, Jr.	----, Billerica, MA
9. Samuel	7 Dec. 1673, Billerica, MA	c.1699, Hannah Hoggett	15 Apr. 1706, Billerica, MA
10. Joseph	14 May 1675, Billerica, MA	-----	25 June 1675, Billerica, MA
11. Enoch	12 Oct. 1676, Billerica, MA	-----	12 Dec. 1676, Billerica, MA
12. Joseph	18 May 1679, Billerica, MA	-----	5 Sept. 1679, ------
13. Elizabeth	13 May 1681, Billerica, MA	-----	16 Dec. 1681, ------

John Trull

b.   *@1634, --------*
m.   *11 December 1657, Sarah French, Woburn, MA*
d.   *15 June 1704, Billerica, MA*

Before 1658, John Trull took up tenancy of the 500-acre farm of magistrate Captain Daniel Gookin's farm, near the mouth of Vine Brook, Billerica, MA. The Shawshin River was on the north of the tract, the town of Woburn to the east. It has been stated that John lived in the Shawshin House, a house built before 1642 and an important location in the community. In 1658, Trull was granted land for his home, a 16-acre plot north of the Commons, west of Pond Street and within reach of the Boston Road. In May 1661, John Trull signed the Parker Agreement allocating 1,000 acres each to Jonathan Danforth and John Parker for laying out another 2,000 acres granted by the Cambridge General Court for the town.

During the Indian uprisings of 1675, the Trull family was assigned to the garrison house of Thomas Patten.

John married Sarah French 11 December 1657, daughter of John French of Cambridge, MA, a brother to William French of Billerica. John and Sarah had 13 children, eight of whom died within six months of their births.

Trull's lifestyle was simple, with practically all of his furnishings homemade. More than one cradle would have been needed in his home. John surely had a large vegetable patch, and depended on hunting wild game, fruit and nuts in all seasons. If he could find a "bee tree" he could have honey for his hominy, made each day as a staple from ground corn. Stew of wild game and vegetables was often eaten for dinner until John acquired a few chickens for eggs and their meat. Fat used in cooking was rendered less from pork, than from bear or possum meat. With the rivers so close to their home, the boys and he could have a few hours of fishing to acquire alewifes, bass and shad with nest or hook and line.

John Trull died 15 June 1704 in Billerica, without a will. His wife Sarah died 26 September 1710.

Pioneers of Billerica • Settling the Shawshine Wilderness: 1654-1660

Founding Father

CHRISTOPHER WEBB
Son of Christopher and Humility Webb; emig. to Braintree, MA before 1645.

m.   ------, Hannah Scott, daughter of Hanah and Benjamin Scott of Braintree, MA.

b. 1635, ------

d. 30 Dec. 1718, Billerica, MA

Children	Born	Married	Died
1. John	23 Oct. 1655, Braintree, MA	1680, Bethia Adams	1 July 1727, Boston, MA
2. Peter	1 Dec. 1657, Braintree, MA	(1) ------, Ruth Bass	12 Feb. 1717/8, Salem, MA
		(2) ------, Amy Hayden	
3. Samuel	28 July 1660, Braintree, MA	1686, Mary Adams	20 Feb. 1738/9, Windham, CT
4. Christopher	25 Jan. 1663, Braintree, MA	1686, Mary Bass	Mar. 1689, Braintree, MA
			Died of smallpox
5. Hannah	5 Sept.1665, Braintree, MA	c.1683/4, John Adams	Apr.-Oct. 1694, Quincy, MA
		A Captain	
6. Benjamin	12 Apr. 1667, Braintree, MA	1692, Susannah Ballentine	Oct. 1739, Quincy, MA
7. Mary	6 Sept. 1669, Braintree, MA	1695, Peter Adams	After 1713, Quincy, MA
		A Captain	
8. Joseph	15 Mar. 1672, Braintree, MA	1699, Deborah Bass	------, Braintree, MA
9. Abigail	13 Oct. 1675, Braintree, MA	------	------

*Four of the Webb children married into the second President John Adams' family

Pioneers of Billerica • Settling the Shawshine Wilderness: 1654-1660

Christopher Webb

b.	*1630, England*
emig.	*before 1645*
m.	*18 January 1654/5, Hannah Scott, Braintree, MA*
d.	*30 May 1694, Braintree, MA*

In 1657, Christopher Webb lived in Braintree, MA and became a Freeman in that community. This recognition signified that he was older than 21 years, attended church regularly, was a good member of society and owned some land. Christopher had been married four years to Hannah Scott of Braintree, the daughter of Hanah and Benjamin Scott.

With the new land opportunities in Billerica, in 1659 Webb acquired a grant of about 72 acres. Today this property is identified with his name at the south side of the village: Webb's Brook. Christopher's house lot was 32 acres, a substantial size for the requirements of his position in society as Gentry. He was often referred to in his lifetime with this title and later with Ensign referring to his position as town clerk.

About six years later, the Webbs returned to Braintree. It could be that Hannah missed her family in that town, or more likely that the Webb Brook's flow of water was not sufficient to set up a dam for a mill. Not only did the stream need a constant flow, but it also had to have a steep enough fall in order to make the wheel turn. In the 17th century, most mills were operated by hand, although horses were brought into use in this period. When Webb acquired his property in Braintree through an Indian deed dated 10 August 1665 for all the east land in Braintree, he built a good-sized dam on the Monatiquit River and set up a corn gristmill. This mill was in use with the Webb name in the 1730's.

The Monatiquit River of Braintree, MA has since been absorbed into usable land for city housing, but remains as a present-day street name in North Braintree adjoining Quincy reservoir, north of the South Shore Shopping Plaza.

Christopher Webb was an energetic, active and learned person, for he had multiple skills as surveyor, town clerk, and attorney in the Suffolk, Middlesex and Essex Counties,

Pioneers of Billerica • Settling the Shawshine Wilderness: 1654-1660

witnessing wills and inventorying personal or family estates. He acquired considerable property through speculation, but also through Braintree Town payments for his surveying.

One of Christopher's activities was to sign the will of Richard Brackett in December 1690, father: of John, Peter, Rachel (Brackett) Crosby and Mary (Brackett) Thompson of Billerica.

In 1680/1, Webb was first noted to be a Selectman, one of the town board elected to execute the affairs of the community. He was considered one of the town's predominant citizens, and on 20 May 1689, he and Joseph Crosby represented their town at Boston to appraise the failure of Governor Andros' governance of the Colony. Issues cited were Andros' demand for taxes without representation, orders for handing over whale oil to the government, because Andros considered whales the crown's fish.

Christopher was related to Mr. Henry Webb, who was the primary member of the Braintree Iron Works. This company failed after an accumulation of debts. In April 1688, Henry died and passed the Iron Works on to Christopher. In order to pay off the financial obligations, Christopher and Hannah deeded their entire property consisting of a corn mill, dam, millpond, one and one-half acres of land with a barn to John Holbrook of Weymouth.

In 1697, Christopher and Hannah's son John reacquired the gristmill for £228, and perpetuated the grinding of corn for 30 more years.

Christopher Webb died in Braintree 30 May 1694, at approximately 60 years of age. He had written his will 14 April 1694, knowing he was near death. The will was probated 28 June 1694 in Suffolk County [13:220]. Christopher wished his wife Hannah to have benefit of their estate during her lifetime, including the white horse. Following her decease, Webb willed his sons John, Peter, Samuel and Benjamin £20 each, son Joseph £40, daughters Abigail Webb, Mary Adams and Hannah Adams £5 each. Peter was to acquire the end of the homestead, in which he already lived.

Webb stated that with son Christopher's death, he wanted this son's children: Christopher, Hanah and Sarah to each have £8. The executors were John, Peter and Samuel Webb. The estate valuation was £385.12.6.

Hannah died in Braintree 30 December 1718. She was 83 years old, having given birth to nine children, six of whom survived her.

Pioneers of Billerica • Settling the Shawshine Wilderness: 1654-1660

Founding Father
SAMUEL WHITING
His parents were Rev. Samuel and Elizabeth (St. John) Whiting
m. ——, Dorcas Chester, ——
    b. 1 Nov. 1637, Wethersfield, CT
    Daughter of Leonard Chester
    d. 12 Feb. 1712/3, Billerica, MA

Children	Born	Married	Died
1. Elizabeth	6 Nov. 1660, Billerica, MA	1702, Rev. Thomas Clark	——, Chelmsford, MA
2. Samuel	19 Jan. 1662/3, Billerica, MA	1686/7, Elizabeth Read	8 Mar. 1714/5, Billerica, MA
3. John	Cornet; captured by Indians and taken to Canada, but escaped 1 Aug. 1664, Billerica, MA Minister, Harvard graduate	——	11 Sept. 1697, Lancaster, MA Killed by Indians
4. Oliver	8 Nov. 1665, Billerica, MA Magistrate, Billerica, MA	1689/90, Anna Danforth	22 Dec. 1736, Billerica, MA
5. Mary	28 May 1667, Billerica, MA	——, John Henry Benchstead (Burchstead)	13 Nov. 1740, Lexington, MA
6. Dorithy	23 Sept. 1668, Billerica, MA	Never married	After 6 May 1723, ——
7. Joseph	7 Feb. 1669/70, Billerica, MA Minister, Harvard graduate	——, Sara Danforth	Before 1712/3, Southhampton, NY
8. James	20 Aug. 1671, Billerica, MA	——	1 Sept. 1671, Billerica, MA
9. Unis	6 Sept. 1672, Billerica, MA	——	20 Sept. 1672, Billerica, MA
10. Benjamin	26 Sept. 1675, Billerica, MA		18 Oct. 1675, Billerica, MA
11. Benjamin	5 Nov. 1682, Billerica, MA		20 Nov. 1682, Billerica, MA

Samuel Whiting ★

Samuel Whiting, Junior, Reverend

b.	*25 March 1633, Skirbecke, Lincolnshire, England*
emig.	*1636*
m.	*2 November 1656, Dorcas Chester, Billerica, MA*
d.	*28 February 1712/3, Billerica, MA*

Samuel Whiting, Jr. was the first minister called to Billerica, MA in 1658. He was not yet ordained, but the town eagerly readied a house with 20 acres of land, promised to help him with chores, and also vowed to pay him £40 a year with possible increments. They wanted him to establish a meeting house, to preach the word of God and understanding of the Bible, and to pray with parishioners in the good times and in times of despair. They also wanted him and his family to become part of Billerica and then remain their pastor. He did so for over 50 years!

Samuel had emigrated to Lynn, Massachusetts in 1636 at the age of three with his parents: Elizabeth (St. John) and Rev. Samuel Whiting, Sr. His father, a true Puritan, had brought his family to this country to found a new Jerusalem, since he was aghast at the religious conflict and turmoil in England. Rev. Whiting, Sr. felt England identified with the Pope and that God had turned against England. To come to America, Samuel Whiting, Sr. and his wife, who was titled, gave up property and wealth.

Samuel, Jr. studied at first with his father in Lynn, MA, and then graduated from Harvard College in 1653. He was ordained in Billerica 11 November 1663.

As with so many ministers throughout the years, it was a challenge for the officers in town to get the church people to pay the minister's salary. It was often in arrears. Somehow, Rev. Whiting, Jr. managed, and was able to increase his land holdings as well. Some of these were gifts.

Pioneers of Billerica • Settling the Shawshine Wilderness: 1654-1660

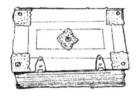

Overall, he had 23 grants of land in Billerica, amounting to more than 200 acres, with the original property on the south side of Charnstaffe at Concord Road. The house stood north of Charnstaffe Lane.

This house was a garrison during the 1675-6 Indian uprising, and was large enough to accommodate his many children. He had married Dorcas Chester 12 November 1656, who was the daughter of Leonard Chester, a nephew of the minister Rev. Thomas Hooker of the Connecticut Valley settlements. Dorcas was born 1 November 1637 in Wethersfield, Connecticut.

One of the greatest contributions Rev. Whiting, Jr. made to the New England church in 1670/1, was to clarify and maintain the separation of church and state when the court wanted to overrule the churches.

Dorcas and Samuel died within days of each other. She died 12 February 1712/3 and he 28 February 1712/3 in Billerica. He left a will [Mdsx. Pro. #24561] written 10 September 1711, when his wife was still living.

In the will, Samuel Whiting, Jr. defined how he wanted wife Dorcas and daughter Dorothy to have use of the homestead and furnishings until after his wife's decease. His son Samuel who was "now in captivity" was to acquire the farm of 400 acres of upland and meadow at Dunstable, valued at £150. Son Samuel was also to be cleared of his debt of "about £100." His son Oliver was to have the land westward of the highway between the barn and the ----- wall at the east end of the English "pastor" to the land of Benjamin Farley, about 18 acres, which Whiting valued at £44. When Dorcas' mother died, Oliver could have acquisition of the old field and English pasture, valued at £22.

Whiting's daughter Mary Burchstead had already received her portion of £90. Dorothy Whiting was to have £80. Another child was listed, perhaps Elizabeth, who married Thomas Clark. The will was most difficult to read and illegible in some parts.

Rev. Whiting, Jr. wanted his books and writings to be used by his children and grand-children, but commented that they may not have been brought up to learn. If his grandson Timothy Clark did learn, he was to have half of his library. A servant, whose name could not be read, was left 40 shillings, and the town of Billerica £3. The executors were Samuel and Oliver Whiting, with Sam Ruggles and Lt. John Sternes nominated to overseer the will. On a final page of the will, Dorothy Whiting was given £80 on 11 March 1713/4.

Pioneers of Billerica • Settling the Shawshine Wilderness: 1654-1660

BIBLIOGRAPHY: Family Lineage

ATKINSON:
Pramberg, Noreen C. Four Generations of the Descendants of John Atkinson of Newbury in 1662. 1985.

BRACKET:
Bracket, Herbert. Brackett Genealogy. Salem: Higginson reprint, 1907.

BROWN:
International Genealogical Index of the Church of Jesus Christ of the Latter Day Saints: Brown of Massachusetts and New Hampshire.

BALDWIN:
Baldwin, John D. Baldwin Genealogies. Worcester, MA: Tyler and Seagrove, 1880.

CROWE:
Crowell, Thomas. John Crowe and His Descendants. Salem: Higginson reprint, 1903.

CROSBY:
Crosby, E.D. Simon Crosby the Emigrant. His English Ancestry and Some of His American Descendants. Salem: Higginson reprint, 1914.

CHAMPNEY:
Watterson, Virginia H. Descendants of the Elder Richard Champney of Cambridge, MA. Carlsbad, CA: 1989.

CHAMBERLAINE:
Glazier, Prentis. The Chamberlain Family of Early New England and New York. Sarasota, FL: 1973.

Trull, James D. The Chamberlain Biography. 1999.

DANFORTH:
May, J.J. Nicholas Danforth of Framlingham, England and Cambridge, New England. Salem: Higginson reprint, 1902.

FARLEY:
Farley, Eugene D. One Line of the Farley Family. Portland, OR: 1991.

Pioneers of Billerica • Settling the Shawshine Wilderness: 1654-1660

Rixford, Mrs. Elizabeth Leach. <u>Families Directly Descended from all the Royal Families in Europe and Mayflower Descendants.</u> Baltimore: Clearfield Publishing, 1932-1999.

Waters, Thomas F. and Eunice W. Felten. <u>Two Ipswich Patriots.</u> Salem: Higginson reprint from Ipswich Historical Society, 1927.

FOSTER:
Hawes, Frank M. <u>An Account of Thomas Foster of Billerica, MA.</u> Boston: F.E. Bradford, 1889.

GRIGGS:
Griggs, Walter S. <u>Genealogy of Griggs.</u> Salem: Higginson reprint, 1926.

GILES:
Vinton, John A. <u>Giles Memorial.</u> Salem: Higginson reprint, 1864.

HUBBARD:
Anderson, Lois H. <u>Hubbard Genealogy.</u> Baltimore: Gateway Pub., 1999.

KEMP:
Weise, Arthur J. <u>The New England Kemps.</u> Salem: Higginson reprint, 1904.

KIDDER:
Stafford, Morgan. <u>The Kidder Genealogy.</u> Salem: Higginson reprint, 1941.

KITTREDGE:
Kittredge, Mabel T. <u>The Kittredge Family in America.</u> Rutland, VT: Tuttle Pub., 1936.

PATTEN:
Baldwin, Thomas. <u>William Patten of Cambridge 1635 and His Descendants.</u> Salem: Higginson reprint, 1908.

PARKER:
Craig, Frances. <u>Some New Hampshire Descendants of James Parker of Woburn.</u> Maryland: 1980.

Parker, Augustus G. <u>Parker in America.</u> Salem: Higginson reprint, 1911.

Parker, William T. <u>Gleanings from Parker Records.</u> Salem: Higginson reprint, 1894.

Richardson, Douglas. "The English Origin and Ancestry of the Parker Brothers of Massachusetts." Boston: New England Historic and Genealogical Society Magazine, January 1999.

POULTER:

Delorey, Janet. "Poulter Family of Raleigh. Essex, England and Billerica, MA." Boston: New England Historic and Genealogical Society Magazine, July 1987.

STERNES:

Van Wagenen, Avis S. Genealogy and Memories of Isaac Stearns and His Descendants. Salem: Higginson reprint, 1901.

SHEDD:

Shedd, Frank E. David Shed's Genealogy. Salem: Higginson reprint, 1921.

SHELDON:

Sheldon, E. Hortense. Sheldons Prior to 1700. Bakersfield, VT, 1961.

TOOTHAKER:

Comtois, Pierre "Lowell Sun" Newspaper. 16 March 1999.

Gregory, Mary I. The Toothaker Family, 1976.

Russell, Donna V. "Roger Toothaker of Plymouth and some Descendants." The American Genealogist. January 1994, Vol. 69:1-2.

Sinnett, Rev. Charles. The Toothaker Genealogy, Brainerd, MN, 1928.

WEBB:

Deiss, Jonathan Webb. The Internet on the Webb Family.

WHITING:

Whiting, William. Memoir: Rev. Samuel Whiting and Wife Elizabeth St. John. Salem: Higginson reprint, 1873.

BIBLIOGRAPHY: Histories, Court and Probate Records

Acts and Resolves of the Province of Massachusetts Bay 1692-1724, Vol. I.

Anderson, Robert C. The Great Migration Begins. Boston: New England Historic and Genealogical Society, Vol. I, II, III, 1995-2003.

Anderson, Robert C., Sanborn, George and Melinda Sanborn. The Great Migration. Boston: New England Historic and Genealogical Society, Vol. I, 1999, Vol. II, 2001.

Batchelloe, Albert S., ed. Probate Records of the Province of New Hampshire. Concord, NH: Rumford Press, Vol. I, 1907.

Bond, Henry. Early Settlers of Watertown, MA. Boston: New England Historic and Genealogical Society, Vol. I, 1860-1981.

Cambridge City Council. Records of the Town of Cambridge 1630-1703. Cambridge, MA. 1901.

Domer, Ronald. "King Philip's Ferocious War." Military History. December 2004.

Essex County, MA. Wills/Probate.

Farmer, John. The Historical Memoirs of Billerica in Massachusetts. Farmer and Brown, 1816.

Green, Samuel A. Groton during the Indian Wars. Salem: Higginson reprint, 1883.

Green, Samuel A. Groton Historical Series 1887-1899. 4 Volumes. Salem: Higginson reprint.

Hammon, Otis G. New Hampshire Court Records 1652-1668. New Hampshire State.

Hazen, Re. Henry. History of Billerica. Salem: Higginson reprint, 1883.

Hotten, John C. Original Lists of Persons of Quality 1600-1700. Baltimore: Genealogical Publishing Co. reprint, 1874-1986.

Hudson, Charles. History of Lexington, MA. Vol. II. Salem: Higginson reprint, 1913.

Massachusetts Historical Society. Early Records. Reel I, pp. 201-2.

Metcalf, Henry H. Probate Records of New Hampshire. Vol. III. Concord, NH: Rumford Press, 1915.

Middlesex County Records, Cambridge, MA.

Middlesex County, MA. Wills/Probate.

Noyes, Sybil, Davis, Walter & Libby, Charles. Genealogy of Maine and New Hampshire. Baltimore: Genealogical Publishing Co., 1979.

Otis, Amos. Genealogical Notes of Barnstable Families. Vol. I & II. Baltimore: Genealogical Publishing Co. reprint, 1888-1991.

Paige, Lucious R. History of Cambridge 1630-1877. H.O. Houghton & Co. 1877.

Paine, Ralph D. The Ships and Sailors of Old Salem. Boston: Charles Lauriat & Co., 1927.

Perley, Samuel. History of Salem. Vol. II, III. Salem: Perley Press, 1926.

Pope, Charles H. The Pioneers of Massachusetts. Baltimore: Genealogical Publishing Co reprint, 1986.

Rapaport, Diane. "Scots for Sale." New England Ancestors. New England Historic and Genealogical Society, Winter 2003.

Savage, James. Genealogical Dictionary of New England. Vol. IV. Baltimore: Genealogical Publishing Co. reprint, 1981.

Schutz, Eric R. & Tongias, Michael J. King Philip's War. Woodstock, VT: Countrymen Press, 1999.

Smith, Leonard. Cape Cod Library. Vol. II. Baltimore: Genealogical Publishing Co., 1002.

Stratton, Eugene A. Plymouth Colony Its History and People. Salt Lake City: Ancestry Publishing Co., 1986.

Suffolk County, MA. Wills/Probate.

Syvret, Marguerite and Stevens, Joan. Balleine's History of Jersey. London: Phillimore, for Societe Jersiase, 1998.

Tepper, Michael, ed. "Founders of New England." Immigrants to the Middle Colonies. Baltimore: Genealogical Publishing Co., 1979.

Torrey, Clarence A. New England Marriages Prior to 1700. Boston: New England Historic and Genealogical Society, 1992.

Willison, George F. Saints and Strangers. Orleans, MA: Parnassus, 1945.

Worthen, Edwin B. Tracing the Past in Lexington, MA. NY: Vantage Press, 1998.

BIBLIOGRAPHY: Salem Witch Trials

Fowler, Samuel P. Salem Witchcraft. Salem: H.P. Ives and A.A. Smith, 1861.

Hill, Frances. Hunting for Witches: A Visitor's Guide to the Salem Witch Trials. Commonwealth Editions, 2002.

Hill, Frances. The Salem Witch Trial Reader. Da Capo Press, 2000.

Jameson, J. Franklin. Narratives of the Witchcraft Cases. New York: Barnes & Noble, 1914.

Roach, Marilynne K. The Salem Witch Trials. Cooper Square Press, 2002.

Robinson, Enders A. The Devil Discovered. Hippocrene Books, 1991.

Robinson, Enders A. Salem Witchcraft Genealogy. Maryland: Heritage Books, 1992.

Starkey, Marian L. The Devil in Massachusetts. Anchor Books, 1989.

Upham, Charles. Salem Witchcraft. Higginson reprint, 1959.

Woodward's Historical Series; Records of Salem Witchcraft. Vol. II.

BIBLIOGRAPHY: Vital Statistics, Massachusetts

Andover
Barnstable
Billerica
Boston
Braintree
Cambridge
Charlestown
Chelmsford
Concord
Dunstable
Essex
Gloucester
Groton
Ipswich
Lexington
Marblehead
Newbury
Plymouth
Salem
Scituate
Woburn

Index of Names of Persons

About The Author

Growing up in New Jersey, Shirley Moore became familiar with many historical landmarks, battlefields, and significantly, her own family history. Both of her parents' families had come to America in the earliest years of colonization and been involved in the Dutch, English and German settlements, the Revolution, piracy, church building, and many varieties of farming. Family beliefs and values were repeatedly emphasized, with the central theme of respect and concern for others and the world in which we live.

She graduated from Douglass College in 1952 and received her master's degree in social work at the University of Pennsylvania. Her keen interest in mental health and family history led her to a career in psychotherapy and to the development of community programs to help troubled people live their own lives with more control over their problems.

Shirley had a 48 year marriage with William E. Barnes and with him had three children. Along with her interests in antiques, crafts, embroidery and painting, she traveled frequently. After training at the Smithsonian in conjunction with the National Genealogical Society in 1980, she started on her journey of genealogical research. Since then she has written books on the families: Barnes, Currin/Cubbon, Van Nuys and Baird, and Moore/More with her brother, Dr. George Moore.

The author moved to Billerica, Massachusetts from Vermont in 2003 and immediately became interested in the history of Billerica and its founding fathers. After extensive research, these are their stories.

.